P9-CPX-111

Praise for *The Grace of God*

"Andy Stanley has captured grace with a wide-angle lens . . . and it is one beautiful sight."

—BETH MOORE, FOUNDER OF LIVING PROOF MINISTRIES

"Andy Stanley on grace: how could you NOT want to read it? Andy is one of the most compelling voices of this generation. He doesn't just know about grace; he lives it."

—JOHN ORTBERG, AUTHOR AND PASTOR OF
MENLO PARK PRESBYTERIAN CHURCH

"Grace is a foundational pillar of our faith, and understanding it is essential for every believer. Andy Stanley's *The Grace Of God* is an amazing, in-depth study of grace, and his contemporary style really allows you to understand how amazing God's grace really is."

—JOYCE MEYER, BEST-SELLING AUTHOR
AND BIBLE TEACHER

"Andy Stanley has done it again! He has taken a subject that many of us think we know a lot about and reminded us that God's grace is greater than we could ever fully know or completely understand. What a great book that takes us even deeper into that "Amazing Grace!"

— MAC POWELL, LEAD SINGER OF THIRD DAY

KoK

The
GRACE
of
GOD

The

GRACE

of

GOD

ANDY STANLEY

THOMAS NELSON
Since 1798

NASHVILLE DALLAS MEXICO CITY RIO DE JANEIRO

© 2010 by Andy Stanley

All rights reserved. No portion of this book may be reproduced, stored in a retrieval system, or transmitted in any form or by any means—electronic, mechanical, photocopy, recording, scanning, or other—except for brief quotations in critical reviews or articles, without the prior written permission of the publisher.

Published in Nashville, Tennessee, by Thomas Nelson. Thomas Nelson is a trademark of Thomas Nelson, Inc.

Thomas Nelson, Inc., titles may be purchased in bulk for educational, business, fund-raising, or sales promotional use. For information, please e-mail SpecialMarkets@ThomasNelson.com.

Unless otherwise noted, Scripture quotations are taken from HOLY BIBLE: NEW INTERNATIONAL VERSION®. © 1973, 1978, 1984 by International Bible Society. Used by permission of Zondervan Publishing House. All rights reserved.

Scripture quotations marked AMP are from THE AMPLIFIED BIBLE: OLD TESTAMENT. ©1962, 1964 by Zondervan (used by permission); and from THE AMPLIFIED BIBLE: NEW TESTAMENT. © 1958 by the Lockman Foundation (used by permission).

Scripture quotations marked MSG are from *The Message* by Eugene H. Peterson. © 1993, 1994, 1995, 1996, 2000. Used by permission of NavPress Publishing Group. All rights reserved.

Scripture quotations marked NASB are from NEW AMERICAN STANDARD BIBLE®, © The Lockman Foundation 1960, 1962, 1963, 1968, 1971, 1972, 1973, 1975, 1977, 1995. Used by permission.

Scripture quotations marked NLT are from *Holy Bible*, New Living Translation. © 1996. Used by permission of Tyndale House Publishers, Inc., Wheaton, Illinois 60189. All rights reserved.

Scripture quotations marked TNIV are from HOLY BIBLE, TODAY'S NEW INTERNATIONAL VERSION® TNIV® Copyright © 2001, 2005 by Biblica®. All rights reserved worldwide.

ISBN 978-0-8499-4693-6 (IE)

Library of Congress Cataloging-in-Publication Data

Stanley, Andy.
  The grace of god / Andy Stanley.
    p. cm.
  Includes bibliographical references.
  ISBN 978-0-8499-4814-5 (hardcover)
  1. Grace—Biblical teaching. 2. Grace (Theology) I. Title.
  BS680.G7S73 2010
  234—dc22

                                2010029335

Printed in the United States of America
10 11 12 13 14 15 RRD 7 6 5 4 3 2

For Mary Gellerstedt:
You saw the future when others
could not see past the moment.

Contents

Acknowledgments

While most books have individual authors, no book is the product of individual effort. *The Grace of God* is certainly no exception. To begin with, this book wasn't even my idea. Matt Baugher, vice president and publisher with Thomas Nelson, suggested the topic. He recognized *grace* as a theme in my preaching that had never been a primary theme in my writing. When I reminded him of all the great books already written on this subject, he quickly reminded me of how long ago those books were published. He had a point. So we went to work. Thanks, Matt.

Matt's second contribution to this project came by way of an introduction. I mentioned to Matt that I needed someone who could help me organize my material and create a strong first draft. He said he knew just the guy. Matt introduced me to Mark Gaither. Mark is a freelance writer from Dallas who is a published author in his own right. I liked Mark immediately. I started sending him MP3s and outlines, and in return he began sending me completed chapters. Mark's insight into the Scriptures, his commitment to biblical scholarship, and his love for excellence ensured that this project would exceed my best effort. Thank you, Mark.

The other two individuals who were instrumental in getting this project across the finish line are Suzy Gray and Diane Grant. Suzy serves as my agent, and Diane is my ministry assistant. Suzy, thank you for riding herd on the details. Thank you for reading and rereading and then reading again. Your relentless commitment to quality is reflected in the finished product. When I wanted to be *done*, you wanted the book to be better. Thanks for pushing.

I'm constantly telling leaders that the key to their success is for them to only do what only they can do. For that to happen, a leader must have someone in his professional world who can keep the path clear of unnecessary distraction. For me, that someone is Diane Grant. Diane and I have worked together for more than twelve years. Directly or indirectly, she's involved in everything I do professionally. And this book is no exception. Diane, thank you for tracking down what must have felt like an endless list of outlines. Thank you for managing communication between all the various parties involved. Thank you for discovering and setting up Dropbox. And thank you for handling all the stuff I don't know about because you decided I didn't need to know about it. That's what you do best. It's no wonder that so many pastors send their assistants to sit at your feet to learn.

Lastly, I want to thank the members and attendees of North Point Community Church, Browns Bridge Community Church, and Buckhead Church. So much of what I've learned about the grace of God I've learned while serving alongside you these past fifteen years. Thank you for creating churches that unchurched people love to attend, churches where the grace of God is not just talked about but modeled and celebrated.

The Story of Grace

Grace.

It's what I crave most when my guilt is exposed. The very thing I'm hesitant to extend when I'm confronted with the guilt of others—especially when their guilt has robbed me of something I consider valuable.

Therein is the struggle, the struggle for grace. It's this struggle that makes grace more story than doctrine. It's this struggle that reminds us that grace is bigger than compassion or forgiveness. This struggle is the context for both. When we are on the receiving end, grace is refreshing. When it is required of us, it is often disturbing. But when correctly applied, it seems to solve just about everything. Contrary to what is sometimes taught, the opposite of grace is not law. As we will discover, God's law is actually an extension of grace. The opposite of grace is simply the absence of grace.

To say that someone *deserves* grace is a contradiction in terms. You can no more deserve grace than you can plan your own surprise party. In the same way that planning voids the idea of surprise, so claiming to *deserve* voids the idea of grace. You can ask for it. You can plead for it. But the minute you think you deserve it, the *it* you think you deserve is no longer grace. *It* is something you have earned.

But grace can't be earned.

To earn something is to find an equivalent. There is no equivalent where grace is concerned. Grace is birthed from hopeless inequity. Grace is the offer of exactly what we do not deserve. Thus, it cannot be recognized or received until we are aware of precisely how undeserving we really are. It is the knowledge of what we do not deserve that allows us to receive grace for what it is. Unmerited. Unearned. Undeserved. For that reason, grace can only be experienced by those who acknowledge they are undeserving.

From the beginning, the church has had an uneasy relationship with grace. Yet history has shown that the church and Christianity in general fare best when characterized by grace. The church is most appealing when the message of grace is most apparent. Yet grace is often an early casualty in the world of organized religion. The gravitational pull is always toward graceless religion. Instead of defining itself in terms of what it stands for, the church often takes the less imaginative and easier path of defining itself in terms of what it is against.

The odd thing is that when you read the New Testament, the only thing Jesus stood against consistently was graceless religion. The only group he attacked relentlessly was graceless religious leaders. So we should not be surprised when we get to the end of the Gospels and discover that the people who crucified him were those who claimed to know God but knew little of grace. In doing so, they confirmed everything he said about them.

As we are about to discover, grace is not a New Testament idea. Grace didn't begin with Jesus. But it was certainly personified by him. John tells us that he was "full of *grace and truth*" (John 1:14; emphasis added). Not the balance between, but the embodiment of. John speaks of "the fullness of his grace" (1:16), the idea being that in Jesus we get as clear and as close a look as we will ever get of what grace looks like in an otherwise graceless world.

In Jesus there was no conflict between grace and truth. It is that artificial conflict that throws so much of Christianity into disarray. It is our misunderstanding of grace, as modeled and taught by Jesus, that leaves us feeling as if grace allows people to "get by" with things.

But grace doesn't dumb down sin to make it more palatable. Grace doesn't have to. **Grace acknowledges the full implication of sin and yet does not condemn.**

Grace is understood best within the context of relationship. After all, it is only within the mystery and complexity of relationships that grace is experienced. So it seemed to me that the best way to approach this subject would be to simply tell the story of grace. It is a story that begins in the beginning. It is a story that traces its way through every book of the Old and New Testaments.

The story of grace includes a broad range of characters—rich, poor, powerful, and powerless. In each chapter, we will parachute into the life of a biblical character at a time when his or her future hung in the balance. For all of them, it is God's grace that tips the scale in their favor. In the process we will discover that in some ways these stories are our stories. For like the individuals who populate the pages of Scripture, we, too, need grace.

But not just any grace.

The grace of God.

CHAPTER 1

In the Beginning, Grace

*Grace has been the basis of our relationship
with our Creator from the very beginning.*

Fiist-time Bible readers are often struck by the apparent contrast between the God we discover in the Old Testament
and God as explained by Jesus in the New. To be candid,
even people very familiar with the Bible often struggle with this contrast. Several years ago, my wife, Sandra, studied the Old Testament
as part of a course that required students to read straight through
the historical books, Joshua through 2 Chronicles. Like many long-
time Christians, she grew up with a devotional approach to Bible
reading, so most of the better-known stories were familiar. But she
had never read straight through the narrative portions of the Old
Testament.

Early one morning I walked in on her while she was reading,

and she looked up at me and said, "I'll be glad when I'm finished with this."

"Really?" I said. "Why?"

She shook her head and said, "This isn't how I view God. Basically, he condones genocide."

Genocide. That term had recently taken on new meaning for us. Three months earlier we had visited Rwanda. We talked to survivors. We visited the genocide museum in Kigali. Horrific photographs and video footage of the carnage revealed the evil that had plunged this African country into darkness for one hundred days, during which at least five hundred thousand men, women, and children were slaughtered. Piles of bodies, mass graves, heaps of skulls. Children who survived were left orphaned and homeless. We also saw the instruments of destruction. The drunken civilian death squads known as *Interahamwe* preferred the machete, a weapon that created carnage of Old Testament proportions.

After experiencing that somber, haunting place, we cannot speak the word *genocide* without feeling sick. Sandra was right. The parallels were too obvious to ignore.

In his book *The God Delusion*, noted atheist Dr. Richard Dawkins declared,

> The God of the Old Testament is arguably the most unpleasant character in all fiction: jealous and proud of it; a petty, unjust, unforgiving control-freak; a vindictive, bloodthirsty ethnic cleanser; a misogynistic, homophobic, racist, infanticidal, genocidal, filicidal, pestilential, megalomaniacal, sadomasochistic, capriciously malevolent bully.[1]

But he isn't the first to draw such conclusions. In the second century, Bishop Marcion was so struck by the contrast between descriptions of God in the Old and New Testaments that he concluded they must refer to different beings altogether. He believed the God of the Old Testament created the physical world and introduced the Law, which was based on retribution, through Judaism. Whereas Marcion characterized the Old Testament God as a cruel and jealous Lawgiver, he saw the New Testament God as a compassionate and loving Father who was concerned about all mankind. He believed this New Testament God revealed himself through Jesus Christ.

While the church in Marcion's day considered his teaching heretical and eventually excommunicated him, one can't help but appreciate his attempt to reconcile the apparent contradictions between God as presented in the Old and New Testaments; the God of war versus the kinder, gentler God who sent his Son to redeem the world from sin.

With all that in mind, it would seem that a study of grace should begin with the gospel of Matthew. On the surface, it appears that the birth of Jesus signaled the beginning of an age of grace. However, a careful reading of the Old Testament reveals grace to be God's preeminent characteristic from the very beginning. So that's where our journey will begin. In the beginning.

⁓◦

The Old Testament opens with an explanation of how the world came to be. While modern readers immediately dive into the details surrounding the process of creation, the author had far more in mind. Shortly after the Israelites escaped the bonds of slavery in Egypt, Moses wrote this remarkable book as a means of introducing them to God. After more than four hundred years of exposure to Egyptian mythology and a polytheistic worldview, the Israelites' collective memory of God had become distorted. So the first three chapters of Genesis represent far more than just the story of creation.

This was Israel's introduction—or reintroduction—to the God of their fathers. This was their glimpse into the nature and even the personality of *the* God, who had singled them out as his people. After what they had just witnessed—their miraculous departure from Egypt, the parting of the Red Sea, astounding displays of God's power over people and nature—not a soul among them doubted his ability to create something out of nothing.

They were not looking for an explanation for how things came to be as much as they wanted to know who had delivered them and who they were being asked to follow.

According to the creation accounts of other ancient religions, the gods took up residence in a preexisting universe. They didn't create the world; they merely ran it. But Moses claimed that the Hebrew God existed before anything. He brought all matter and time into existence out of nothing—not because he had to but, apparently, because he wanted to. And that's where we encounter the very first expression of God's grace.

Philosophers and scientists have been wrestling with a fundamental question for generations: *Why does anything exist at all?* Or, another way of asking it: *Why is there something rather than nothing?* Not to worry, we aren't going to spend too much time here. But this question deserves to be explored before we examine the familiar story of creation. It is impossible for us to imagine *nothing*. But apparently there was nothing before there was something. In the past, some scientists suggested that matter might be eternal. But more recent investigation suggests that matter, space, and time each had a beginning. Something came from nothing. But why? Why something? Why not nothing?

Assuming you believe in God, let me ask this question a different way. *Why did God create anything?* Some argue that he was lonely, but I don't think so. Even if that were the case, an argument could be made that the act of creation was an extraordinary act of grace. God created life, which created the potential for you and me. Creation gave you an opportunity to *be*. And God was under no obligation to give you or me that opportunity. Why is there something rather than nothing? Because God decided there should be something. And part of that something is you! **In the beginning God created, and this was a marvelous act of grace. But that was just the beginning.**

Moses wrote that after creating time, space, and matter, the universe was "formless and empty." Into this void God said, "Let there be light," and there was light. Then God commented on his creation: "God saw that the light was good, and he separated the light from the darkness" (Gen. 1:2–4).

The Creator isn't the only one who views light as something good. You do as well. And so do I. But God was under no obligation to create light. The world could have been left in utter darkness and we would never have known the difference. Have you ever thanked God for light? Me neither. We take it for granted. The only time I stop to express gratitude for light is when our electricity is restored after an ice storm. But within minutes I slide right back into my take-it-for-granted frame of mind. We don't generally consider the creation of *light* as an extension of God's grace. But if you have visually impaired friends, you know that the miraculous restoration of their sight would certainly be a cause of thanksgiving and that no one would consider it far-fetched to credit God for his *grace* on their lives. The difference? Light is a constant for the average person. Light is not a constant for those who are visually impaired. God's 24/7 extensions of grace generally go unnoticed, until they are taken away. And even then, our appreciation and recognition last only a short time.

The remainder of the creation story describes how God

systematically brought order to a "formless and empty" universe. He divided the sky from the earth, the dry land from the waters, the day from the night. He dotted the heavens with the sun, moon, planets, and stars to measure the passing of time. He filled the earth with life—endless in variety, boundless in scope, relentless in resilience, marvelous in complexity. None of this was necessary. God was under no obligation to go to these seemingly great lengths. But he did. And at every juncture, at the end of each creation cycle, we find a phrase that gets little attention yet declares the grace of God in a subtle but powerful way: "And God saw that it was good" (vv. 10, 12, 18, 21, 25).

I think most people take that to mean that God looked at his handiwork and thought to himself, *Nice job!* You know, the kind of thing you would say to yourself after painting a room in your house or washing your car. *That's good.* Sounds a bit silly when you stop and think about it. "God saw that the light was good" (Gen. 1:4). Like he didn't know it was good until he paused to look at it? Like it was an experiment? Or perhaps instead of patting himself on the back, he said it in a comparative sense. Perhaps he had tried this before and it wasn't so good, but this time he got it right.

I don't think so. Neither does anybody else I've read.

Another option suggests that creation was good in a moral sense. But that doesn't really work either. Dry land isn't morally good or bad. It's just dry land. But God declared it good. Strange, isn't it? Good for what? Good for whom? Good for God? Did God benefit from the division of the land from the sea or from the creation of birds and fish?

By the time God finished, more than three hundred species of beetle populated the earth. Was all of that for his sole benefit and enjoyment? Did it really matter that the seed-bearing plants would reproduce after their own kind? Was it for God that certain plants were created for food and others just for their beauty? Would God, who is spirit, benefit from either? In other parts of the Scripture, we discover that all of creation declares God's glory (Ps. 19:1). But who hears this declaration?

You; that's who. And me.

God declared each phase of creation good because it was good for *us*.

Not sure you buy that? Sound a little self-serving? Hang on, because what happens next sheds some light on all that had come before.

"Then . . ." (Gen. 1:26)—as in, after everything was ready. "Then"—as in, after the stage was set. "Then"—as in, after God got everything the way he knew we would need it to be. "Then God said, 'Let us make human beings in our image, to be like us.' . . . So God created human beings in his own image. In the image of God he created them" (Gen. 1:26–27 NLT).

And what did God do with them? He told them to enjoy themselves. Everything he had painstakingly fashioned, he created for them. Here's how Moses described it. Take special note of the words I've emphasized:

> Then God said, "I *give* you every seed-bearing plant on the face of the whole earth and every tree that has fruit with seed in it. They will be *yours* for food. And to all the beasts of the earth and all the birds of the air and all the creatures that move on the ground—everything that has the breath of life in it—I *give* every green plant for food." And it was so. (Gen. 1:29–30; emphasis added)

God created the world, filled it with goodness, and then gave it away. He handed us the keys. He created a world perfectly suited to sustain the human race. What did we do to deserve this incredible, pristine abundance? Nothing. Absolutely nothing.

That's grace. From the standpoint of human experience, the creation of the universe and God's giving it to humanity was the beginning of grace. Majestic sunsets—those are for you. The seasons that enable us to plant and harvest—those are for you. The variety of fruits and vegetables you have enjoyed throughout your life—those are for you. Your choice of salmon, sea bass, trout, or snapper—that's for you. The beach, the mountains, the lakes, the streams, the rainforest, the jungles, the plains—all for you. There is more beauty in this world than any one person can fully comprehend, greater abundance than any one person can consume. Why? That's the nature of grace. **Grace is never *just enough*. Grace is always far more than enough.** From the very outset, God established his pattern of lavishing grace upon those he loves. But the best was still still to come.

~~~~~~◠)

In the midst of all that God declared good, one thing did not please him: "The LORD God said, 'It is not good for the man to be alone'" (Gen. 2:18).

Once again we are confronted with God's unending commitment to, and love for, humankind. Why create a woman? Because it was not good for man to be alone. We see from the very beginning of creation that God desires what is good for us. That's grace. Undeserved favor. God wanted, and continues to want, only what is *good* for us. For you. When he saw that humanity was incomplete, he acted. "I will make a helper suitable for him" (Gen. 2:18). Why? Because he had to? No, the text is clear. Because he wanted to.

"So God created human beings in his own image. In the image of

God he created them; *male and female* he created them" (Gen. 1:27 NLT; emphasis added).

It would be a mistake to rush by this too quickly. Why male and female? Why not just create a big electronics store full of males? Why not create a big outlet mall and fill it with females? We would have never known the difference. But apparently God would have known. So he created man and woman. In doing so, he created a capacity for love and intimacy that Adam, on his own, would never have experienced. He created the experience of sexual fulfillment. He created the potential for children and the unique love that only a parent can comprehend. With the creation of man *and* woman came the ability to enjoy life in its fullest expression. And why did God push his creative capacity to such an extreme? Because he wanted to. Maybe here, more than anywhere else in the Old Testament, God reveals his feelings toward humankind. He wants what is good for us, so he filled creation with endless extras.

God blessed Adam and Eve with an abundance of everything they needed to thrive, and he encouraged them to enjoy life to the fullest. He filled the garden with lavish varieties of food, not merely to sustain but to delight. He gave the couple each other and the gift of sexual relations, not merely to procreate but to savor the joys of unblemished intimacy. And then he gave them one more thing: something to do.

Adam and Eve were guided to a particularly lush part of God's newly formed world, and there he did two remarkable things, things he didn't do for any other created being. He blessed the couple and gave them responsibility. God said, "Be fruitful and increase in number; fill the earth and *subdue* it. *Rule* over the fish of the sea and the birds of the air and over every living creature that moves on the ground" (Gen. 1:28; emphasis added).

God gave Adam and Eve a purpose for living. Purpose. That's just one more aspect of God's grace. He granted them second-in-command status as his vice-regents over all of creation. And along with that authority, he gave them the responsibility to subdue the earth. Put simply, they were to extend and maintain the order he had given the world. But he didn't give them any real guidelines. In fact, there was really only one rule. "From any tree of the garden you may eat freely; but from the tree of the knowledge of good and evil you shall not eat, for in the day that you eat from it you will surely die" (Gen. 2:16–17 NASB). Lots of "yes" trees; just one "no" tree.

Isn't that interesting? In the beginning, there was a lot of responsibility and only one rule. When God had the world just the way he wanted it, there was just one commandment.

Once again, we bump into a seemingly insignificant aspect of creation that we may be tempted to overlook. Depending upon how you were raised and the church you did or did not attend, this may be a critical juncture in your understanding of God's grace in your life. In the beginning there was no guilt. In the beginning there was no condemnation. In the beginning the first two people never went to sleep at night wondering where they stood with God. **Whereas God's expressions of grace were innumerable, his requirements were minimal.**

That tells us a lot about God. That's a lesson life has a way of erasing pretty quickly. A lesson rarely underscored in the way we are raised. That's an insight difficult to keep front and center within the complexity of our current religious systems. You may have drawn the very opposite conclusion. Perhaps from your perspective, God's requirements are innumerable and his grace minimal. If that is the case, you are not alone. You are in the majority. And my hope is that by the time you reach the halfway mark in this book, you will have shed much of that misbelief and will embrace God as he is: the God characterized by grace.

In the beginning there was more beauty than mankind could absorb. In the beginning there was more food than could be consumed. In the beginning there was purpose. In the beginning there was intimacy free of intrigue and suspicion. In the beginning there was uninterrupted fellowship between God and humanity. And in the beginning there was freedom. Freedom to decide. Just as God was under no compulsion to create and provide, so mankind was under no compulsion to receive and reciprocate God's love. Grace in its purest form can have no strings attached.

This fragile system fueled by grace and gratitude hinged on an even more fragile ideal: trust. God completely trusted mankind with his creation. Every day Adam and Eve chose whether or not they would be trustworthy with this responsibility. And for a while they were. How long, we do not know. We do know, however, that eventually man violated God's trust, and everything changed. Everything.

~

Much of our confusion around grace stems from our confusion about sin. Simply put, we *severely* underestimate the impact of sin on our souls and on our world. I'm not sure we can fully grasp the significance of what happened when sin entered the world. According to the Genesis account, all of creation was affected. Everything under mankind's authority, which was pretty much everything, was poisoned by sin. The apostle Paul would look back on this hinge point in history and write that all of creation was subjected to "decay" and "corruption" (Rom. 8:21 NIV, NASB).

Our problem is that this corrupted world is all we know. So while from time to time we are bothered by what we see around us, upset by the way things are going, or frustrated that things are not like they used to be, we really have no idea of how bad it truly is. Do fish know they are wet? Do polar bears know how cold it really is? Do the Cape Range Blind Fish (who spend their entire lives in the underground lakes of the Australian Outback) know they can't see? Like all of creation, we've adjusted to our surroundings. We are cognizant of the fact that there are variations in the degrees of evil in the world. But since a broken world is all we've ever experienced, we can't begin to appreciate how far things are from the way God intended them to be.

In American culture, we've substituted the term *mistake* for the terms *wrong* and *sin*. We aren't sinners; we are really just *mistakers*. How many times have we heard prominent leaders describe their extramarital affairs as *mistakes*? A mistake is something you make while balancing your checkbook. A mistake is an accident. Unless both parties were blindfolded and gagged, I don't think it's possible to have an accidental affair. And, of course, once discovered, public apologies are made to family members and constituents who were hurt by what happened. But if you do something you know is going to hurt someone, is that still a mistake? The people who were hurt rarely think so. But in a world that's far from the way God intended it to be, *sin* is reduced to a *mistake*.

So for reasons we will never understand, Adam and Eve were not content to eat from the abundance of the "yes" trees. They felt compelled to eat the fruit from the one tree God said was off-limits. And in that moment, sin entered the world. Immediately they became aware of their nakedness and were ashamed. How interesting. Sin was the gateway to shame. In the beginning, *shame* served a purpose. But shame is another casualty of a sin-filled world. In our culture it is something to be avoided. Shame is another one of those things we work so hard to erase from culture. After all, what purpose could it possibly serve?

Along with shame, there was another immediate consequence of sin: impaired judgment. Exhibit A: Adam and Eve tried to hide from

God. They tried to hide from God in the garden *he* created. How bright was that? About as bright as our trying to avoid God by avoiding church. But God played along with Adam and actually asked, "Where are you?" (Gen. 3:9). God knew where Adam and Eve were. But apparently they didn't. And if you've read the story, you know that it just went downhill from there. Sin led to shame. Shame led to blame. Adam began to make excuses for his behavior and actually blamed God for what he did. "The woman *you* put here with me—she gave me some fruit from the tree, and I ate it" (Gen. 3:12; emphasis added). Translated: "If you hadn't put this woman in my life, none of this would have happened!"

And in that moment, something very significant began. Don't rush past this. If you highlight phrases in the books you read, highlight this next one. **In the beginning Adam blamed God for his troubles, and mankind has been blaming God ever since.** From our vantage point, we can see what's really going on. Adam is simply refusing to accept responsibility for his behavior. And when anyone refuses to accept responsibility for his behavior, he goes looking for somebody to blame. Adam chose God. So do we.

We have all struggled to reconcile the realities of suffering and injustice with the idea of a sovereign and just God. And from Genesis forward, God has taken the rap for all that is evil in this world. "The woman you put here with me . . ." becomes *The accident you allowed to happen. The disease you refused to heal. The break you refused to give me.* And on and on we go. But just as Adam's rationale was flawed, so is ours.

How did God respond to all the blame and the shame? Grace. He gave Adam and Eve precisely what they did not deserve. It could even be argued that he broke his own promise in order to give them what they did not deserve. They were warned that on the day that they ate of the tree of the knowledge of good and evil, they would die (Gen. 2:16–17). But they didn't. Growing up, I was told that they died *spiritually*. But that's not part of the story. I was told they were separated from God. But that's not in the story either. In fact, right after they sinned, Adam and Eve had a long conversation with God. It wasn't the most positive conversation we find in the Scriptures, but God didn't suddenly disappear from their lives. Their sin did not cause them to be unable to hear his voice. And their sin did not so separate them that God couldn't or wouldn't come looking for them. As we've already seen, God made the first move: "Adam, where are you?"

God patiently listened as Adam and Eve tried to shift blame and escape responsibility for their sin; then he pronounced a series of curses. The original Hebrew text sets the passage in the form of poetry.

> *To the woman he said,*
> *"I will greatly increase your pains in childbearing;*
> *with pain you will give birth to children.*
> *Your desire will be for your husband,*
>   *and he will rule over you."*

> *To Adam he said, "Because you listened to your wife and ate from*
> *the tree about which I commanded you, 'You must not eat of it,'*
> *Cursed is the ground because of you;*
> *through painful toil you will eat of it*
> *all the days of your life.*
> *It will produce thorns and thistles for you,*

and you will eat the plants of the field.
By the sweat of your brow
you will eat your food
until you return to the ground,
since from it you were taken;
for dust you are
    and to dust you will return." (Gen. 3:16–19)

In response to the couple's sin, God cursed the woman to suffer anguish in childbirth and the man to endure toil in earning a livelihood. He cursed the couple's intimacy so they would experience strife. He even cursed the ground. Seems awfully harsh, doesn't it? But hey, Adam and Eve didn't die. God had every right to wipe the slate clean and start from scratch. But instead, he granted them mercy in the form of curses.

Merriam-Webster defines *mercy* as "compassion or forbearance shown especially to an offender or to one subject to one's power, *also*: lenient or compassionate treatment."[2] God demonstrated mercy by holding back the swift, final administration of justice that Adam and Eve had earned through their disobedience. Instead, he delayed their physical death, buying time—as it were—to put into place a plan of redemption. Instead of destroying Adam and Eve for their sin, God cursed them and their offspring so they would live with the consequences of their wrongdoing.

To curse in Hebrew means "to surround someone with obstacles" or "to render someone powerless to resist." In this sense, every good parent has *cursed* his or her child from time to time. To a child all discipline feels like a curse, but to the parent, it's a way to teach two important lessons: *disobedience* has consequences, and *obedience* leads to freedom. God responded to Adam and Eve's sin like good parents respond to their children: he disciplined them. For their sake and the sake of future generations, he disciplined them. And his discipline was an expression of *grace* for them and *grace* for those who would follow. Every parent with multiple children eventually comes to understand this. To let an older child get away with creating chaos in the home is an invitation to the younger sibling to follow suit. To allow an older sibling to get away with creating chaos in the home is to refuse to protect the other kids in the home. So God chose not to destroy but to discipline. In this way, grace came into a world that would henceforth be characterized by sin and death.

Thousands of years later, a New Testament writer would come right out and say it: "The Lord disciplines those he loves" (Heb. 12:6). This is the other side of grace. I don't discipline other people's children. They are not my responsibility. I am the greatest threat to the children I love the most. I am the only dad that comes to mind when they think, *I hope my dad doesn't find out.* But I am also the only father they run to when they are scared, hurt, or in need. And so it is no surprise that no sooner had God thrown Adam and Eve out of the garden than he turned right around and gave them something they would need in this new world of shame, something to wear: "The LORD God made garments of skin for Adam and his wife and clothed them" (Gen. 3:21).

There it is again. Grace. **From the very beginning God has responded to the sin of humanity with . . . well . . . amazing grace**. And I've skipped the most surprising expression of all. After outlining the consequences of Adam and Eve's behavior, God addressed the serpent and foreshadowed the coming of one who would take the full brunt of sin's penalty on behalf of the human race:

So the LORD God said to the serpent,

"Because you have done this,
Cursed are you above all the livestock
and all the wild animals!

You will crawl on your belly
and you will eat dust
all the days of your life.
And I will put enmity
between you and the woman,
and between your offspring and hers;
he will crush your head,
    and you will strike his heel." (Gen. 3:14–15)

The woman's offspring in this case represents all of humankind, as she and Adam become fruitful and multiply. This announcement of divine discipline predicts that all of humanity will continue to endure the affliction of evil. But there's a hint of something more profound in the last two lines of this first curse: "*he* will crush your head." The word *he* is a singular pronoun. A bit strange in this context. If "he" referred to the human race, it should have been plural. Apparently God wasn't referring to the human race in general, but to one particular "he"—the second Adam, he who would come in the name of the Lord with the authority to lay down his life on behalf of the sins of mankind. He who would endure the affliction of evil and suffer the penalty of death that Adam was promised and we all deserve. Here, in this dramatic transition from a world we can only imagine to the world we know, we find the promise of grace personified, grace that will one day enable us to reenter a world where sin is no more and death is undone.

In the beginning there was grace. But that was just the beginning!

CHAPTER 2

Chosen by Grace

Because of grace, God chose to clean up what we messed up.

Have you ever been responsible for cleaning up a mess that's so big you don't know where to begin? I once dropped a large glass jar of salsa in our pantry. The instant it left my hand, I knew what I would be doing for the next hour or two. When the jar hit the floor, chunks of tomato, pepper, and glass exploded in every direction. Sauce oozed down the three walls and the inside of the door. Red polka dots covered every surface—cereal boxes, cans, other jars of salsa, my legs . . . I remember stepping out of the pantry, closing the door, and saying to my wife, "Sandra, I think it's time to sell the house and move." I felt the same way when Shadow, our Lab, knocked down a shelf full of paint cans, and a couple of gallons of oil-based paint poured out onto the basement floor. Where do you even start?

Having waded into several situations like that, I've learned a secret. When it comes to cleaning up a colossal mess, you just have to pick a place to start and then start. Otherwise, it's just too overwhelming.

It's impossible for us to imagine how God must have felt when he looked at the mess sin had made of creation. Everything had been corrupted. Nothing remained untainted. A perfectly balanced ecosystem designed to meet the needs of every uniquely created organism, contaminated. Contaminated by the very ones assigned to protect it! The author of Genesis tells us,

> The LORD saw how great man's wickedness on the earth had become, and that every inclination of the thoughts of his heart was only evil all the time. The LORD was grieved that he had made man on the earth, and his heart was filled with pain. (6:5–6)

Soon afterward, God flooded the world, destroying all those who refused to believe in him. Only one small band of believers, Noah and his family, responded to God's invitation to be delivered from the judgment that would come. And so the earth was destroyed by water.

One would assume that a fresh start would solve the problem created by sin. But sin is like a virus, and humanity had been infected. The birth of each newborn spread the infection further, and within a few generations, the earth teemed with rebellious men and women. The sin God hates and the humanity he loves are so intertwined that to destroy one is to destroy the other. Yet to spare humanity would mean the epidemic of sin would consume the world.

So God had a mess on his hands—a mess of epic proportions. Rather than wade in and clean it up, God could have chosen to do nothing. Perhaps it crossed his mind to simply shut the pantry door and sell the house. If that was an option, it was an option he did not choose, fortunately for us. He chose instead to extend grace to a graceless world. **God chose to wade in hip deep and clean up the mess sin had created.** The ultimate solution was a Savior—a Savior whose redeeming work would create a way for God to eradicate sin without destroying his people. But where could he begin the process of redemption in a world where sin tainted everything? He really only had one choice.

He began with a sinner: Abram.

In ancient times, nations and families worshipped territorial gods, deities associated with a particular region. Conquering nations gave thanks to their god (or gods), while conquered civilizations questioned theirs. God opted to leverage this worldview to his advantage.

God would begin with a nation, a nation chosen by him to demonstrate his power and goodness to the rest of the world. This nation would receive his favor as part of a one-sided covenant in which he obligated himself and demanded nothing in return. The Lord would initiate this covenant as an expression of his grace, not in response to any merit of theirs. He would promise to nurture and to preserve this nation forever. He would treat this nation like a son, rewarding obedience and chastising rebellion. He would settle this nation at the crossroads of the ancient world so that the merchants and armies of all nations would carry compelling tales of a remarkably advanced civilization and the invisible God they served. This nation would be the mouthpiece through which he would speak to the world, offering salvation to all who would believe in him and receive his grace.

Unfortunately, all the existing nations and civilizations on the earth were taken. They already had laws and superstitions that shaped their ideology. The existing people groups had carved their reputations in the minds of their neighbors through pagan ceremonies and cultic practices informed by values that were in direct opposition to what God intended at creation. So rather than reform an existing nation, the Lord God decided to start his own. He would create a new nation—an entirely new people group. And rather than beginning with a tribe or even a family, God decided to start with an individual. This was certainly not the quickest route to nation building. But it was the only route in light of the consequences of sin and the redemptive purposes of God. He would establish a covenant with one man of his choosing, whose offspring would multiply and in time become a nation. In this way, every member of this new nation would become an heir to the covenant God established with his or her ancestor. They would all be, as it were, sons and daughters of a new covenant.

So God selected Abram. He plucked from the cradle of ancient civilization an ordinary, unknown member of an idol-worshipping society. But Abram was not just any man. He was an old man! He was in his seventies. And to complicate things further, his wife had given him no children. She was barren. Not the most ideal couple with which to launch a nation!

This was where God decided to begin cleaning up the mess sin had made. He determined to begin a nation through a man with no influence, no children, and no homeland. God said to Abram, "Leave your country, your people and your father's household and go to the land I will show you" (Gen. 12:1). And then, for no reason other than he just wanted to, God made Abram a threefold promise.

> *I will make you into a great nation*
> *and I will bless you;*
> *I will make your name great,*
> *and you will be a blessing.*
> *I will bless those who bless you,*
> *and whoever curses you I will curse;*
> *and all peoples on earth*
> *will be blessed through you.* (Gen. 12:2–3)

When God initiated his relationship with Abram he began with a promise—a promise Abram did not deserve or ask for. This was all God's idea. The Lord didn't issue Abram a set of behaviors to adhere to. The Ten Commandments wouldn't appear for several generations. He simply asked Abram to receive *promises*. This invitation for Abram to trust him was how God initiated their relationship. As we will discover throughout the remainder of this book, that's exactly how God has been initiating relationships ever since.

~~~

God asked Abram to follow him to a new land. So Abram and his entourage, consisting of servants and some extended family, lived the nomadic life of tent dwellers. They tended enormous flocks, which they moved from place to place to find the best pastures, and they cultivated unclaimed land, raising enough food to feed themselves and sell to the city dwellers.

Abram grew wealthy and remarkably powerful despite the instability and vulnerability of nomadic life, but the inability to put down roots took its toll after more than a decade. Several scrapes with death unnerved the aging, childless patriarch. Abram had demonstrated astounding courage in the face of evil, and he had exercised heroic trust in the Lord's protection more than once. But after one particularly close brush with danger, Abram sat in the doorway of his tent, examining the cuts and bruises covering his body. His feet—blistered and bloody from ninety miles of double-time marching, close-quarters fighting, and then a hurried return home—throbbed and burned like never before. A dull ache penetrated every muscle and radiated from every joint. As his wife, Sarai, and a servant tended his wounds, Abram began to feel his age and the taste of bitter irony filled his mouth. He was homeless in the land given to him by God.

This was just one irony in a lifetime of ironies. His parents had given him the name Abram, which means "exalted father," yet with his eightieth birthday well behind him, he hadn't fathered an heir. Sarai had long since made peace with her barrenness, so the childless patriarch began to wonder how God would fulfill his promise ("I will make you into a great nation"). Maybe so. But they were running out of time.

With his wounds bound and his feet wrapped in healing herbs, Abram lay his wearied body down for a long sleep. Sometime during the night, the Lord appeared to him in a dream. God said, "Do not be afraid, Abram. I am your shield, your very great reward" (Gen. 15:1).

Abram replied, in effect, "I want to believe you, but I don't have much evidence to rely upon—at least not in the tangible sense. You say I will be the father of a great nation, but I'm an old man and my wife is an old woman, and the only heir I have is Eliezer, my chief of staff."

The Lord very patiently reassured Abram. He didn't scold him or even rebuke him. Instead he declared, "This man will not be your heir, but a son coming from your own body will be your heir" (Gen. 15:4). Then God told Abram to look into the cloudless night sky. "Count the stars—if indeed you can count them. . . . So shall your offspring be" (Gen. 15:5).

As Abram stared at the black canopy of space littered with billions of stars, he made a critical choice. He decided to believe God. Despite the lack of tangible evidence and in spite of his working knowledge of human reproduction and the effects of age on procreation, Abram placed his trust in God's character. He believed in the Lord's integrity to follow through on his promises; Abram trusted God's power to accomplish the impossible.

And then something remarkable happened.

In response to Abram's faith, God declared him righteous (v. 6). God said, in effect, "Because you have trusted in me, I give you the gift of righteousness. I have written *forgiven* across your moral ledger sheet. Because of your faith, I have cleared your account of all debt." **At that very moment, the Lord established an important precedent: a righteous standing with God comes through faith.** This is the single most important aspect of God's grace.

God called Abram to trust him, and despite his sin, Abram found peace with God through faith. As soon as Abram believed in God, the Lord formalized his one-sided contract with his chosen man. In a ceremony that would have been very familiar to Abram, God committed himself to Abram's provision and protection in the same manner a powerful king pledges provision and protection to a subordinate ruler. Only in this case, the contract required nothing in return.

During the ceremony, God revealed the future to Abram. He said, "Know for certain that your descendants will be strangers in a country not their own, and they will be enslaved and mistreated four hundred years. But I will punish the nation they serve as slaves, and afterward they will come out with great possessions" (Gen. 15:13–14). The Lord then granted Abram and his descendants a vast tract of land with a detailed description of its boundaries.

Now, as incredible as all that must have been for Abram, there was still the issue of Sarai not being able to have children. Abram *believed* God's promises, but nothing actually changed. In time, Abram and Sarai began to doubt his promise. Their bodies weren't getting any younger. In the silence, they began to scrutinize the Lord's words, wondering if perhaps they had mistaken his meaning. After all, God had promised Abram "a son coming from your own body" (Gen. 15:4), but he said nothing about Sarai being the mother. Perhaps thinking the Lord needed some help getting the plan in motion, Sarai offered a suggestion. "The LORD has kept me from having children. Go, sleep with my maidservant; perhaps I can build a family through her" (Gen. 16:2).

As offensive as this is to our twenty-first-century, Western way of thinking, this sort of arrangement was not all that uncommon in ancient times. So Abram followed his wife's counsel and fathered a boy, named Ishmael. But instead of making things better, it made things much worse. Instead of bringing blessings, Abram and Sarai experienced the curses of envy, conceit, rivalry, bitterness, and cruelty. The maidservant flaunted her ability to conceive, which prompted Sarai to retaliate. Eventually, Abram banished the woman and her son from the camp, causing them to face the wilderness alone, where the rejected pair almost died.

Finally, more than fifteen years after God's covenant ceremony, a couple of lapses of trust, and one giant mistake, the Lord met the aging man with exciting news. Abram, at ninety-nine, and Sarai, approaching ninety, would conceive and bear a son within a year. It was then that God gave them new names. Abram, "exalted father," became Abraham, "father of a multitude." Sarai became Sarah, "princess."

Soon afterward, however, before Sarah's belly began to bulge, Abraham moved his tent compound to a new territory, not far from the city of a powerful king. Fearing someone from the city would notice Sarai's beauty, he lied. When asked, he said, "She is my sister." Once again his plan backfired. The king decided to honor Abraham by marrying his "sister." And again, the Lord intervened by exposing Abraham's cowardly lie, prompting the king to confront Abraham. "What have you done to us? How have I wronged you that you have brought such great guilt upon me and my kingdom? You have done things to me that should not be done" (Gen. 20:9).

The irony of a pagan king lecturing God's chosen man on the

need for integrity could not have been lost on Abraham. How could a man who had been promised so much trust so little? Why would a man who had been protected by God in miraculous ways fear a mere king? And no doubt in the back of Abraham's mind was the nagging fear that perhaps his breach of faith would forfeit God's promises. This incident, along with the attempt to fast-track an heir, was certainly reason enough for God to renege on their deal. But as Abraham was discovering, he didn't really have a deal with God. Instead, he was the recipient of an unconditional promise. And a few months after the Lord's announcement, the couple welcomed their first and only child into the world—a son, whom they named Isaac.

We will never know for sure, but perhaps God waited to fulfill his promise until after Abraham had ample time to prove through his behavior that he was unworthy of such an honor. If God's gift of righteousness was conditional, Abraham certainly provided God with an out. But God was not looking for a way *out* of his covenant. Just the opposite. With the birth of Isaac, he had just taken another step toward creating a path back *in* for humanity.

⁓

Despite Abraham's failure, God's plan progressed. He was building a nation one person at a time. Abraham finally had a legitimate heir. No doubt, Abraham and Sarah savored every moment with their son. He had become the literal embodiment of God's promise to Abraham and to all of humanity. Through him God would multiply his grace. Through this boy all the nations in the world would be blessed. God was on the move. Granted, he was moving a bit slowly for Abraham. But at least he and Sarah had gotten a son in the process.

At least for a while.

Once again God spoke to Abraham. "Take your son, your only

son, Isaac, whom you love, and go to the region of Moriah. Sacrifice him there as a burnt offering on one of the mountains I will tell you about" (Gen. 22:2).

Child sacrifice was not uncommon in those days. But sacrificing one's only son certainly was. Especially a son promised to you by God and given in old age. This didn't make any sense. But the Scripture tells us that Abraham didn't hesitate to obey. He rose early the next morning to obey God's ominous instructions. The cool air of morning must have stood in sharp contrast to the tempest in Abraham's heart. Doubts, fears, sorrow, confusion, and anger must have swirled like an Arabian sandstorm as he led his only son into the wilderness to die. The journey took the patriarch, his son, and two servants into the mountains of southern Canaan. It would take them three days to reach their destination. Three days for Abraham to change his mind. Three days to plead with God to change his.

The specific purpose of child sacrifice varied from culture to culture, but generally it was an attempt to appease temperamental gods. We can only guess as to the meaning Abraham would have attached to this dreaded deed as they made their way up the mountain. Was this punishment for his previous faithlessness? Was Isaac paying for his father's disobedience? Was this a test? Would God take this son and provide another? Had God changed his mind altogether? By the time this incident occurred, Abraham had been walking with God for many years. In some ways that must have made all of this even more confusing. On the other hand, God had made him a promise. So Abraham decided to trust.

As they neared their destination, Abraham ordered the two servants, "Stay here with the donkey while I and the boy go over there. We will worship and then we will come back to you" (Gen. 22:5). Abraham could see the confusion on Isaac's face as the two started out with wood, a knife, and a torch, but no animal to sacrifice. "The fire and wood are here," Isaac said, "but where is the lamb for the burnt offering?" (v. 7).

There's no way to appreciate the range of emotions that must have swept through Abraham at that moment. Hoping that God might change his mind, he responded, "God himself will provide the lamb for the burnt offering" (v. 8). Abraham had no idea how true those words would prove to be, not only in his immediate context, but in the context of God's grand plan for the redemption of the world. God would indeed provide the lamb.

Abraham gathered stones, constructed an altar, and arranged the wood on the surface. Then he bound his son with cords, picked him up, and laid him on the wood. The terror in Isaac's young eyes must have been more than Abraham could bear. He pulled the knife from its sheath to end his son's life, just as he would a sacrificial lamb. But before the blade touched the boy's skin, God intervened. From everywhere and nowhere, a voice called, "Abraham, Abraham!"

"Here I am," he replied.

The angel of the Lord said, "Do not lay a hand on the boy. . . . Do not do anything to him. Now I know that you fear God, because you have not withheld from me your son, your only son" (Gen. 22:12).

No doubt Abraham's hands were trembling as he cut the cords binding his son. As Isaac's feet touched the ground, a commotion in the undergrowth caught their attention. Just a few feet away, a ram struggled to untangle its horns from a thicket.

God had provided.

~~~ෙ

Abraham died at the age of 175. By that time, Isaac, the first son of the covenant, had fathered two sons of his own. But Abraham's name had not become great. The families of the earth had not been blessed through him. He had not taken full possession of the land he was promised. But in time, through his descendants, all of that would come to pass. Not because of anything extraordinary on Abraham's part, but because God made a promise—a promise Abraham believed.

And with that, the cleanup had begun. The mess sin had created was being addressed. God's plan of redemption was unfolding. And the common thread throughout the story was grace. Because of grace, God chose Abraham. By grace he declared him righteous. By grace God provided for and protected Abraham and his family, even when they disobeyed. It was God's grace that moved him to bless Abraham and Sarah with a son. And it was God's grace that would move him to see this story through to completion.

The importance of God's interaction with Abraham cannot be overemphasized. In Abraham, God established the relational ground rules for all mankind: **a right standing with God comes through faith in the promises of God.**

Hundreds of years before God gave the nation of Israel the Ten Commandments, God gave Abraham the gift of righteousness. His message could not have been clearer: the solution to sin was not rule keeping. If it had been, God would have begun the cleanup process with a list. Instead, he initiated a relationship. He asked an undeserving man to trust him. And when that man did, God gave him what he needed most and deserved the least—friendship with God (James 2:23; 2 Chron. 20:7). That's amazing.

What's even more amazing is that the offer of friendship God made to Abraham would eventually extended to the entire world. This offer would be made on the same terms: *trust me*. But in a world where sin reigned, the simplicity of this offer was easily lost. This is understandable. Men and women in every culture know they fall short of God's standards. Our consciences make that unmistakably clear. Common sense argues that if bad behavior puts us at odds with God, then good behavior should fix things. Our natural inclination is to *do something* in order to regain God's acceptance and approval. So throughout the history of civilization, people have devised every imaginable system and scheme to please their god or gods. But when the one true God initiated his relationship with mankind, it didn't begin with a command; it began with an invitation: will you trust me?

Hundreds of years later, one of Abraham's descendants would find himself in a bitter debate with other descendants of Abraham over the question of how one attains a right standing with God. While those he debated appealed to the Law of Moses as the standard by which righteousness was attained, the apostle Paul would reach farther back into their rich history and appeal to the story of Abraham:

> It was not through law that Abraham and his offspring received the promise that he would be heir of the world, but through the righteousness that comes by *faith*. . . . Therefore, the promise comes by *faith*, so that it may be by *grace* and may be guaranteed to all Abraham's offspring—not only to those who are of the law but also to those who are of the faith of Abraham. (Rom. 4:13, 16; emphasis added)

The only way to clean up a giant mess is to pick a spot and begin. God began with an ordinary man. He offered that man what everybody needs most: peace with God. In making that offer, God offered hope to the human race. By embracing the faith of Abraham, mankind could be reconciled to God. The separation sin created could be bridged after all, but not through any scheme created by men—only by the grace of God. With Abraham, the story of reconciliation began. It's a story of forgiveness and redemption—a story that would continue for hundreds of years. A story that would eventually become your story and mine.

CHAPTER 3

Surprised by Grace

Grace is not reserved for good people;
grace underscores the goodness of God.

No doubt you are familiar with the idea of sowing and reaping. Somewhere along the way you've heard someone say, "You reap what you sow." Other ways of stating the same thing include:

You get what you have coming.
What goes around comes around.
Actions have consequences.

Like all principles, the principle of sowing and reaping can work for you or against you. Felonies result in prison sentences. Academic diligence results in good grades.

This cause-and-effect principle is foundational to human experience. And it is taught and illustrated in both the Old and New Testaments. We can only assume that God established this principle at the same time he established the law of gravity and other laws of physics. The idea behind any principle is that it makes certain components of life relatively predictable. That's a good thing. I would hate to get to retirement and discover that a penny saved is a penny lost. Or worse, that there was a way to double my carb intake, while avoiding exercise, and still maintain my suggested weight and waistline. As it stands, I'm under the impression that the principle of sowing and reaping determines the relationship between what I eat and what I weigh.

As we discovered in chapter 1, sin wreaked havoc with everything in creation. So while the principle of sowing and reaping continues to be operational in our world, there are exceptions. And I bet you already knew that. Like me, you've seen some hardworking, responsible people who did everything right financially fall on hard times because of circumstances completely beyond their control. You know people who took great care of themselves whose bodies were eventually destroyed by disease. I bet you've seen some dishonest people prosper too.

But the good news is that there is another kind of exception to the principle of sowing and reaping. This one is not the result of the brokenness caused by sin. This exception is the result of God's love and his mercy. The exception I'm referring to is *grace*. Just as sin sometimes results in bad things happening to good people, so grace creates the possibility of good things happening to undeserving people. The presence of *sin* means that sometimes we don't get the good that we deserve. The presence of *grace* means that sometimes we don't get the consequences we deserve. **Grace is the vehicle God uses on occasion to ensure that we get precisely what we don't deserve.** Moved by love, he turns the world's capricious cruelties into divine opportunities for "good" people, and he even uses the evil intentions of "bad" people to redeem them.

Perhaps no story in the Bible illustrates this particular expression of God's grace better than a tale of two brothers. Joseph, an uncommonly good man, suffers unspeakable injustice, while Judah, a wily, callous hypocrite, enjoys undeserved prosperity and popularity. As it happens, God had a plan for both of them.

Jacob, the grandson of Abraham, fathered twelve sons with four different women. Unfortunately, he did little to hide the fact that Rachel was his favorite wife and that he loved her two sons, Joseph and Benjamin, more than the other ten boys combined. He shamelessly doted on Joseph, sparing him the most difficult chores and showering him with special gifts, including a spectacular multicolored tunic. His colorful cloak became a vivid daily reminder to the other boys that they would never earn the kind of love Joseph received so freely.

While Joseph later proved to be a supremely good man, he wasn't perfect. In fact, he didn't do himself any favors in how he treated his brothers. The family raised sheep and goats as part of their agrarian existence, and back then, shepherds often led their flocks to the greenest pasture they could find, even if it took them several days' journey from home. Joseph, at the age of seventeen, took it upon himself to become his father's eyes and ears, informing on his older brothers when they didn't manage the flocks well.

One evening, as Joseph and his brothers sat around a campfire, perhaps with the sound of bleating in the background, he stirred the coals with a stick and casually said, "I had an interesting dream last night."

"Oh really? What about?" one replied.

"About all of you. We were working in grain fields, binding the stalks of grain into bundles when, all of a sudden, my bundle rose from the ground and stood up straight and tall. Then your bundles got up from ground, surrounded mine, and bowed down to it. How 'bout that? Strange, huh?"

The brothers didn't miss the significance of Joseph's dream. "So you think you're going to reign over us, do you?"

As time passed, their resentment festered into a seething hatred. They could barely speak to him without cursing. Joseph, oblivious to his effect on others, continued to share his dreams.

"Hey, I had another interesting dream," he announced. "In this one, the sun, the moon, and eleven stars were bowing down to me. What do you think of that?"

Outraged, his father asked, "What are you saying? That at some time in the future your mother and I will bow before you, along with your brothers?"

Joseph offered no answer. His brothers gnashed their teeth and suppressed the urge to tear him to pieces. His father, however, tucked away the dream and pondered it from time to time. Jacob knew something about dreams. He had experienced a number of visions that made no sense at the time but eventually came true.

Hatred is rarely a passive thing, more than mere emotion. Hatred is nothing less than murder waiting to happen. Only fear of getting caught keeps hate-filled people from bringing a despised person to a sudden end. So several months later, when Jacob sent his favored son to check up on his brothers, Joseph found them ready to kill.

The ten brothers had taken the family's flocks about sixty miles north to a lush valley in present-day Galilee. The baby of the family, Benjamin—also favored by Jacob—was too young to leave home, so Joseph traveled alone through rugged wilderness to find his family's flocks. When he appeared on the horizon, the men sneered, "Here comes the dream master!" and unanimously agreed that this day would be his last. They planned to kill him and dump his body into a pit, where scavengers would devour every trace of his existence. That way, they could tell their father the truth: Joseph had been eaten by a wild animal. After all, a half-truth isn't a complete lie, right?

But the oldest brother, Reuben, talked the others out of killing Joseph. "Throw him into the pit alive. If we let him die on his own, we won't have his blood on our hands." He secretly planned to rescue Joseph later but let the others think what they wanted. They reluctantly agreed. So when Joseph arrived, the ten brothers pounced on the favored son, stripped the multicolored tunic from his body, and threw him into a dry cistern, a deep hole carved out of stone to collect rainwater.

While Joseph's cries for help echoed from the nearby hole in the ground, the brothers shared a meal and debated what to do next. About that time, a caravan of traders rolled across the valley, their camels loaded with merchandise for sale in Egypt. And that's when Judah emerged as a leader among the brothers. Unlike the oldest brother, Reuben, who hoped to rescue Joseph and return him safely home, Judah found a way to compound their sin and make a little cash as well. The caravan gave him an idea.

"Guys, I've been thinking. We shouldn't kill Joseph. After all, he *is* our brother. Besides, if we just kill him, we'll have a big mess on our hands and we don't gain anything. But if we sell him, he's gone from our lives *and* we pocket some silver in the process. It's the perfect solution!"

Judah veiled his greed beneath a thin veneer of mercy. In the years to come, he would perfect that skill to become a master of disguise.

The men pulled Joseph from the cistern, turned him over to the slave traders, divided the silver ten ways, and watched the caravan disappear over the southern horizon, never expecting to see their dreaming brother again. And there it is: the principle of sowing and reaping gone awry. The good kid gets thrown in a pit and sold into slavery, and the evil brothers profit by it. And if you know the story, you know it gets even worse.

For the brothers, the only unanswered question at this point was what to tell dear ol' dad. A splash of goat's blood on little brother's multicolored tunic and a few convincing rips would be all the alibi they needed. "Joseph must have fallen prey to wild animals somewhere between home and our encampment. We didn't even find his body. All we found was his tunic." With their well-rehearsed story, they broke their father's heart.

Perhaps it was in that moment that it dawned on them that their treachery would never be completely behind them, for their father's grief would serve as a continual reminder. In the ensuing years Judah and his brothers would be forced to carry their secret. Long after the money was gone, the memory would remain. And who knows—perhaps Judah regretted his role as the mastermind of the conspiracy. But if so, there was never any evidence. As Jacob's intense anguish gave way to an ever-present melancholy, Judah maintained an innocent exterior, perhaps even feigning concern when called upon for comfort. In time, Judah mastered the skill of hiding his true, private self behind an honorable, public facade. And so the wicked prospered while the innocent suffered.

The biblical narrative follows Joseph to Egypt, where he became a central character in the story of Israel's history. While there, he was falsely accused of attempted rape and sentenced to hard time. Nevertheless, he maintained a tight grip on his integrity, and eventually, God lifted Joseph above his circumstances to establish him as a leading national figure in Egypt. Meanwhile, Judah's story went from bad to creepy.

With Joseph out of the picture, Judah moved on with his life. He relocated to a town several miles from home, married a local woman, settled down, and started having kids. He fathered three boys: Er, Onan, and Shelah. When Er grew to be a man, Judah arranged his marriage to a woman named Tamar. Unfortunately for her, Er proved to be such an evil man that the Lord ended his life early (Gen. 38:7). This left the young woman widowed and childless, a desperate situation in those days.

Ancient cultures had a tradition called *levirate marriage* that protected childless widows from poverty and destitution. According to this custom, one of the dead man's relatives could claim his estate, marry his widow, take care of her, and father children with her. Usually, this would be a brother, but in Canaanite law, any eligible relative could fulfill this duty. So, in keeping with custom, Tamar married Er's brother Onan, but he also did what was displeasing in the sight of the Lord and died (Gen. 38:10), which put Judah's third son, Shelah, next in line.

At this point, Judah saw a pattern. Two sons married Tamar and promptly died. According to the Bible, they died as a result of their own evil, not because of Tamar. Nevertheless, Judah wasn't eager to send a third son to suffer the same fate as Er and Onan. He could have refused to fulfill his family's obligation by forbidding the marriage, but he had a reputation to keep. His peers would never excuse such a huge break with custom, and his community would have labeled him an irresponsible, untrustworthy scoundrel. A man who would not care for his family could not be trusted to honor his business contracts, and he certainly couldn't be trusted with public office.

Judah surveyed the situation and found a convenient loophole in the custom. Shelah, the third son, was too young to marry. So Judah approached Tamar with a compromise. He said, in effect, "Until Shelah is old enough to marry, conduct yourself like a grieving widow: live with your father, wear the customary widow's garments, and reject all other proposals of marriage. Don't worry, I'll take care of you in due time." It sounded reasonable on the surface and helped Judah maintain his honorable public persona, but it was a vow he never intended to fulfill. He hoped everyone would forget the agreement as the years passed.

Eventually, Shelah grew to adulthood and became eligible for marriage. Meanwhile, Tamar had faithfully fulfilled her part of the agreement; but Judah showed no signs of honoring his promise. In fact, when Judah's own wife died, he could have fulfilled his obligation to Tamar by marrying her himself, but he did nothing. And by this time, Tamar found herself in a very vulnerable position: older and with fewer childbearing years left. She would not have the same opportunities for marriage as before. If her father died, she would have no means of support. So she decided to take matters into her own hands.

Each spring, wealthy men left their homes to personally oversee the harvest of wool and to enjoy a time of celebration. Wine, wool, and women put rich men in an agreeable mood, so if you were going to collect a debt or ask someone to fulfill an obligation, this was the time and place. But Tamar didn't intend to ask Judah for anything. She knew better than to rely on his integrity. Instead, she planned to give Judah a dose of his own deception.

She took off her widow's garments and dressed herself like a temple prostitute. Canaanite sheep-shearing festivals often involved cultic prostitution and pagan rituals to enhance fertility for the coming year, and Tamar knew Judah's habits. She sat in the gateway of the little town near the shearing festival, knowing Judah would be there. In those days, influential men of the community sat near the main gate of a city, where they made business deals and decided legal matters.

Tamar's veil prevented Judah from identifying her, and he certainly would not expect to find his daughter-in-law dressed like a temple prostitute. The fact that he didn't recognize her during the conversation also says something about their interaction over the years. Clearly he had not stayed in touch to check on her welfare or to reassure her. Regardless, Judah solicited her services and they agreed that the price would be a goat. (Apparently, that was the going rate for that sort of thing three thousand years ago.)

Of course, Judah didn't have the goat with him; he would have to send one back to her later. However, Tamar knew better than to trust Judah's promise. Before agreeing to sleep with him, she demanded a deposit, something of value she could hold until he returned with payment. She asked for two items: Judah's signet, a bronze stamp worn around the neck and used to seal business transactions; and his staff, an ornately carved, utterly unique personal possession. In today's terms, this would have been like asking someone to leave his driver's license or social security card as a guarantee.

Judah agreed.

A few days later Judah fulfilled his promise and sent the goat by way of a servant. But the mysterious prostitute was nowhere to be found. Tamar had put on her widow's garments and returned home, leaving Judah's proxy no way to find her. He asked the men of the town where he might find the temple prostitute who sat by the gate, but they said, "There has been no temple prostitute here."

When this was reported to Judah, rather than embarrass himself and risk becoming the butt of town jokes, he decided to let the matter go. He would return home after the festival, order a replacement signet, carve a new staff, and forget the whole thing happened.

Three months passed. Judah's life returned to business as usual while Tamar kept to herself. But as spring blossomed into summer, Tamar's tummy began to bulge. Before long, people began talking. Eventually local gossip reached Judah. His daughter-in-law had "played the harlot" and she was pregnant!

Judah responded exactly like someone hiding a secret sin, someone pretending to be someone he's not. He burned with "righteous indignation" against the sin of another while conveniently forgetting his own wrongdoing. He became the quintessential self-righteous judge, taking the public downfall of Tamar as an opportunity to conceal his own hypocrisy. He said, "My daughter-in-law has shamed my family. Let her be tried publicly and burned alive for her sin!"

How righteous Judah must have felt. How his neighbors must have sympathized with this pillar of their community as he endured the disgrace brought upon his house by Tamar. How utterly proper for him to defend his good name against the shame of his daughter-in-law's sin!

But the duplicity of his response would be laughable if it wasn't so tragic. Isn't this the same Judah who plotted to kill his brother? Isn't this the same Judah who sold his brother into slavery because killing him didn't yield a profit? Isn't this the same Judah who broke his father's heart and let him mourn the death of his son for years? Isn't this the same Judah who promised to take care of his daughter-in-law, never intending to keep his word, and whose dereliction almost forced her into prostitution to avoid poverty?

Knowing the entire story, we see the irony. We know something Judah and his community didn't. Tamar possessed irrefutable evidence of Judah's secret sin. Meanwhile, Tamar remained silent.

On the day set for her execution, men arrived at her home. As these things went, someone would have bound her hands together and shaved her head, and then a mob would have dragged her through the streets to the place of execution. But before any of that could take place, she sent a messenger to Judah. The message was simple: "I am with child by the man to whom these things belong. Please examine and see who this signet ring and cords and staff belong to."

Tamar's plan worked perfectly. By waiting until the last moment, she left Judah nowhere to hide. By this time a crowd had gathered to see Tamar burned for her sin. Judah would be forced to call off the execution and dismiss the charges. In addition, he would be forced to explain his decision. A false allegation of this sort was not a casual matter.

They soon had their answer. Judah had promised to care for his widowed daughter-in-law, yet he never intended to follow through. Judah had used the body of a harlot in secret, yet he publicly condemned his daughter-in-law for behaving like one. To keep herself from becoming destitute, Tamar had to trick Judah into fulfilling his promise.

This whole episode, as strange as it is, finally brought Judah to a turning point in his life. He could no longer hide behind his pillar-of-the-community public persona. He had been exposed as a hypocrite, an idolater, a swindler, and a liar. And he admitted as much to the community who had gathered to burn Tamar as a harlot. His public confession was straight to the point: "She is more righteous than I, inasmuch as I did not give her to my son Shelah" (Gen. 38:26 NASB). Even the bizarre lengths to which his daughter-in-law went to secure her future didn't diminish the fact that her actions were more righteous than his.

Now, if Judah's story ended there, we may be tempted to conclude that he got a *measure* of what he had coming to him. But a short stint of public humiliation compared to almost having his daughter-in-law burned at the stake? It would be hard to make a case that Judah reaped what he sowed. And then there's the whole Joseph scenario. At this point in his life, there were no known consequences associated with that terrible series of decisions. But, as it turns out, Judah's story did not end there.

⁓

Twenty years had passed since the time Judah and his brothers sold Joseph into slavery. He had no way of knowing that Joseph had risen above a series of misfortunes to become the prime minister of Egypt. During Joseph's rise to political power, he engineered a massive government food campaign to store up grain reserves for seven years in order to survive a predicted seven-year famine. Consequently, starving multitudes from all over the Mediterranean world choked the roads and harbors of Egypt, hoping to buy food.

The famine hit Jacob's family especially hard. So hard that he sent Joseph's brothers to Egypt for provisions. He refused to send Benjamin, however. His youngest son was Rachel's only surviving son. Having lost Joseph, he couldn't bear the thought of losing another favored son.

After a dry, dusty journey, Joseph's brothers stood among the throngs of people seeking salvation from the famine. Like everyone else, they appeared before the government official in charge of selling grain to foreigners; that is, the prime minister. However, they didn't recognize their brother. After such a long time, they probably assumed he had died as a laborer in the Egyptian mines. Joseph wore the makeup and official garb worn by all Egyptian officials, and he spoke Egyptian as fluently as a native. Therefore, the ten brothers observed standard protocol when addressing royalty: they bowed. The significance of this moment would not have been lost on Joseph. No doubt time slowed to a crawl as a long-forgotten dream from childhood suddenly consumed his thoughts.

Joseph concealed his identity. He played the part of a suspicious Egyptian bureaucrat in order to test his brothers, to see if they had changed. He also wanted to know if Benjamin had fallen prey to their hatred. So he held Simeon captive and sent the others home with grain, demanding they return with their youngest brother.

Naturally, this didn't go over well with their father, Jacob. He refused to let Benjamin out of his sight; Simeon would have to fend for himself. But with the passing of time, their supply of grain ran low and they would need to make another journey to Egypt. So Judah made his father a vow. "Send the boy along with me and we will go at once, so that we and you and our children may live and not die. I myself will guarantee his safety; you can hold me personally responsible for him.

If I do not bring him back to you and set him here before you, I will bear the blame before you all my life" (Gen. 43:8–9). Jacob finally agreed. He realized that without food, the famine would surely kill Benjamin; but by sending him to Egypt, everyone might live.

When Judah and his brothers appeared before Joseph again, all eleven of them bowed down with respect for this man whose word was law. To their surprise, Joseph hosted an elaborate dinner in their honor. While everyone enjoyed the banquet, Joseph watched his brothers closely, looking for signs of hatred or jealousy for Benjamin. Instead of hatred, he heard sorrow in their voices. They regretted what they had done to Joseph and expressed remorse for the pain they had caused their father.

To be certain of their remorse, Joseph devised one final test. He loaded each man's donkey with as much grain as it could carry, placed the money they had paid back into each man's sack of grain, and then hid an expensive silver cup among Benjamin's provisions. Once their little caravan cleared the city gates, he directed his officials to accuse them of theft and to search them for stolen property. When the Egyptian officials found the silver cup in Benjamin's sack of grain, they promptly arrested him, threatening to keep him as a slave.

Joseph framed Benjamin for the sole purpose of seeing how his brothers would react. Would they sacrifice him to save themselves? Would they take this opportunity to rid themselves of another favored brother? Or would they try to save him?

Judah had personally guaranteed Benjamin's safety with his father, but he was well known for his lack of follow-through. Nevertheless, he asked for a private word with Joseph to plead for Benjamin's release.

Your servant guaranteed the boy's safety to my father. I said, "If I do not bring him back to you, I will bear the blame before you, my father, all my life!"

Now then, please let your servant remain here as my lord's
slave in place of the boy, and let the boy return with his brothers.
How can I go back to my father if the boy is not with me? No! Do
not let me see the misery that would come upon my father. (Gen.
44:32–34)

When Joseph heard this, he couldn't contain himself any longer.
He commanded all of his attendants to leave the court so that only he
and his brothers remained. Until this point Joseph had communi-
cated with his brothers through a translator. Now that they were
alone, the men had to wonder how they would even communicate
with this strange Egyptian. So imagine their shock when he gazed
into their eyes and declared in their own language, "I am Joseph!"
(Gen. 45:3).

Once the recognition was complete, the brothers' heads were bowed
to the ground once again. But this time more out of fear than respect.
And the brother who had the most to fear was Judah. Judah, who
undoubtedly thought of what he would do if the roles were reversed.
Judah, who for more than twenty years had outrun the consequences of
his betrayal. But what goes around comes around. And so he would get
what he had coming to him after all.

But there was no sound of guards rushing into the room. No
clamor of weapons. No orders for arrest. All was strangely calm. This
would be a day Judah would never forget. This was a day of grace. For
on this day he was given precisely what he deserved least. Joseph continued, "And now, do not be distressed and do not be angry with
yourselves for selling me here, because it was to save lives that God
sent me ahead of you" (Gen. 45:5).

This is one of the moments in Old Testament history that I would
have loved to to see for myself. We can only wonder how long it took
for Joseph's words to register. How long before any of the brothers had

the courage to make eye contact? They were consumed with guilt over what they had done. Joseph was consumed with something else entirely. Grace.

Not only did Joseph forgive them, but he invited them to bring their families and to live in the most fertile territory Egypt had to offer. Within seconds, Judah and his brothers went from condemned to death to the position of esteemed guest of the second most powerful man in Egypt. **Once again, the law of sowing and reaping was thwarted. But this time it was thwarted by grace.** As it turned out, Judah never really got what he deserved. As is always the case with grace, he got exactly what he deserved least. But the story doesn't end there.

Years later, as Judah's father, Jacob, lay close to death, his twelve sons gathered around their father to receive his blessing. According to tradition, one would receive a double portion of the estate and bear the title *firstborn*, designating him the official head of the family. Normally, this honor went to the oldest son, the literal firstborn male, but a father could choose anyone at his discretion. By this time, the brothers had accepted Joseph's favored status and fully expected him to become the official patriarch of the family. After all, from boyhood to manhood, Joseph had proven his moral worth in the face of incredible hardships and in spite of unspeakable cruelty at the hands of many people, starting with Judah. He had demonstrated almost supernatural ability as a leader and singlehandedly saved the budding nation of Israel from starvation. If any man had earned the title of firstborn, it was Joseph.

Reuben, the eldest, stepped forward, and predictably, Jacob denied him the privilege. Years earlier, he had insulted the honor of his father by sleeping with one of Jacob's concubines. Reuben nodded in dejected agreement and then stepped back.

Simeon, next in line, stepped forward. He wouldn't receive the birthright either. As an impetuous young man with a violent temper, he and Levi had slaughtered an entire town after the leader's son violated their sister, Dinah. Jacob didn't want the family name to become associated with cruelty.

Levi, having heard his father's indictment against Simeon, knew better than to step forward. Instead, he nudged Judah.

Judah reluctantly approached his father. By now his secrets had become public knowledge. He had masterminded the sale of Joseph into slavery and then callously watched his father grieve his death. And while Joseph lived above reproach as a slave in Egypt, Judah led a double life at home. If any man had forfeited the birthright, it was Judah. But what goes around doesn't always come around.

Judah approached his father and knelt. And here is the blessing he received from Jacob:

> *You, Judah, your brothers will praise you:*
> *Your fingers on your enemies' throat,*
> *while your brothers honor you. . . .*
> *The scepter shall not leave Judah;*
> *he'll keep a firm grip on the command staff*
> *Until the ultimate ruler comes*
> *and the nations obey him.* (Gen. 49:8, 10 MSG)

The insinuation of Jacob's blessing is that Judah's descendants would be kings. This must have struck Judah and his brothers as a bit strange, seeing as they were just a large family, not a nation. Not to mention they were living in Egypt. Yet that is exactly what happened. The families of Jacob's twelve sons eventually became the twelve tribes of the nation of Israel. And beginning with King David, the kings of Israel were born to the tribe of Judah. More significantly, Jesus, Israel's Messiah, was born from the lineage of Judah as well.

Who would have thought?

Judah certainly didn't deserve any of this; his life story reads like a soap opera. Nevertheless, God chose to bring the Messiah into the world through the lineage of Judah, not Joseph. After a lifetime of sin and hypocrisy, Judah was brought to a place of humility and gratitude. But he wasn't brought there through threat of punishment. He was brought there through grace.

In the end, it cannot be said that he found grace. He never went looking for it. On the contrary; grace found him. Through this dramatic story that took more than twenty years to unfold, God continued to weave the theme of grace into the story of mankind. Through Judah's story, we are reminded that **grace is not reserved for good people; grace underscores the goodness of God**.

CHAPTER 4

Redeemed by Grace

The grace of God always precedes the law of God's grace.

One of the most misunderstood relationships in all of Christianity is the relationship between God's law and God's grace. At first glance it's easy to see where there may be tension between the two. After all, if God's law instructs us not to do something and we do it, can we really expect him to overlook our indiscretion because of grace? If he's going to give us what we don't deserve every time, what's the point of giving us any laws?

But the debate between law and grace goes beyond the practical and quickly becomes part of a debate about salvation. There are those who argue that the Law was given to provide us with a way of earning our way into God's good favor, and maybe even earning heaven. Most world religions ascribe to some form of earn-your-way theology. But as I'm sure you are aware, there are a great many Christians who argue that salvation is by faith and grace alone. According to this view, keeping God's law is not a means of earning salvation. But even within the faith-alone camp, I've heard plenty of preachers and evangelists argue that if a person isn't consistently keeping God's law, he isn't *really* a Christian! This take on law and grace implies that keeping the law is proof of salvation by grace. In other words, *real* Christians will obey God's law (at least most of the time). They usually don't consider breaking the speed limit a make-or-break infraction, in spite of what the New Testament teaches about obeying laws instituted by the government. Oh well.

So where does that leave us? The Bible has its share of thou-shalts and thou-shalt-nots. But at the same time, the Bible talks an awful lot about grace. So which is it? Or if it's both, how do they fit together?

Good news. This is not as confusing as people in my profession make it. The easiest way to understand the relationship between God's law and God's grace is to take a look at the most famous list of laws in the history of mankind and the story behind where they came from. The list I'm referring to is, of course, the Ten Commandments.

Most everybody's heard of the Ten Commandments. In fact, most people would agree that we should abide by them. But almost nobody can name them. When I was in graduate school, the dry cleaner I used was operated by a middle-aged woman named Agnes. From time to time I would try and engage Agnes in a conversation about religion. She was quick to remind me that she kept the Ten Commandments. That was her default response to all things religious. And that was also her way of saying that the conversation was officially over! So one day I asked Agnes if she actually knew all ten of the commandments. Without even looking up she said, "No. But I keep 'em."

Agnes is not alone. Just for fun, our church conducted a man-on-the-street-type interview to find out what people actually knew about the big ten. Armed with a camera and microphone, they hit the pavement and asked people to name as many of the Ten Commandments as they could. No one could name them all. Most could name only two. The most astute commandment-keepers could recall only these four:

Do not kill.

Do not steal.

Do not commit adultery.

Do not lie.

No one could remember the first four commandments. Everyone jumped straight to the thou-shalt-not rules of conduct. And that's sad. It's sad because our predisposition toward the thou-shalt-nots supports a universal myth regarding God and his feelings toward the human race. Simply stated: *obedience gets you in, and disobedience keeps you out.* Or another way of saying the same thing is, *God's approval is reserved for the rule followers.* But nothing could be further from the truth.

As rare as it is to find someone who can recite all ten commandments, it is even rarer to find someone who knows the story of how they came to be in the first place. The story is just as important as the commandments themselves. The context surrounding the giving of these commandments resolves the tension we feel between God's law and his grace. As we are about to discover, **the Ten Commandments do not stand in contrast to grace; they are introduced within the story of God's grace**. God's law is featured heavily in the Old Testament, but only as the subtext of a grander narrative that highlights his grace toward a helpless, undeserving group of people.

What follows is the story of the Ten Commandments.

～⌒)

You have probably heard of the promised land, but you may not know where it is or why it's called that. It refers to the land grant portion of God's promise to Abraham that we discussed in chapter 2.

Later, the Lord revealed to Abraham just how his descendants would come to possess the land of promise. He revealed the future in three predictions (Gen. 15:13–16):

1. Your descendants will be strangers in a country not their own.
2. They will be enslaved and mistreated for four hundred years.
3. I will punish the nation they serve as slaves, and they will come out with great possessions.

Sure enough, God's predictions unfolded just as he had said. As we saw in the previous chapter, Joseph saved his family from starvation by relocating them to a fertile valley in Egypt. Abraham's descendants flourished, and after just a few generations, the clan of forty-five multiplied into a nation. Their growing population became a source of great anxiety for a later king of Egypt "who did not know about Joseph" (Exod. 1:8). This pharaoh worried that the Israelites (as they had come to be known) might support an invading army or lead a revolt against Egypt, so he pressed them into slavery. And for many years, perhaps more than three centuries—longer than the United States of America has existed as a nation—forced labor defined the national identity of Israel.

Four hundred and thirty years after Abraham's descendants relocated to Egypt, the nation of Israel had grown to perhaps as many as three million. Yet they had no government; Pharaoh was their king. They had no laws; Egypt ruled over them. They had no land of their own. They knew only captivity, oppression, poverty, and hopelessness. While their bloodline remained pure (Egyptians would never consider marrying slaves), their culture and perspective of God had become tainted with Egyptian superstition.

After four hundred years of slavery, God raised up Moses to lead the Israelites out of Egypt and claim the land he had promised

Abraham. This was Israel's exit from Egypt, which we now call *the Exodus*. These events are described in detail in the second book of the Bible, Exodus.

Soon after bringing them out of Egypt, but before settling them in the promised land, the Lord wanted to define the national identity of the Hebrew people. They needed to know God as their forefathers, Abraham, Isaac, and Jacob (renamed Israel), had known him. Having demonstrated his power in the miraculous events of the Exodus, and having claimed them as his own, purchasing them out of slavery, God gave the Israelites a set of rules to live by. And it wasn't a set of ten rules. The Law of Moses contains more than six hundred rules. There are rules pertaining to diet, sanitation, marriage, children, slaves, animals, and property rights. There are laws defining criminal behavior along with the corresponding punishments. There's a large section of the Mosaic law instructing the nation in the art and practice of sacrifice. If you've ever tried reading the Old Testament book of Leviticus, you may have found yourself wondering, *Why so many laws? Why so much detail?*

Remember, this was a nation of slaves who had never been responsible for themselves. They had no government. No king. No judicial system. No laws. They had Moses and a pillar of smoke that led them through the desert. That was pretty much it. So God gave them a detailed prescription of how to conduct themselves. It's within that framework that we find the Ten Commandments. Apparently these were the first commandments God handed down to Moses. They are high-level laws that set the tone for the laws that followed. When read in context, one thing becomes abundantly clear: these ten laws, along with the six hundred that would follow, had absolutely nothing to do with where anyone spent eternity. God was simply establishing behavioral guidelines for a group of people who had none. But not just any group. A group he had redeemed from slavery. A group he had already established as his own.

~~~

You can tell a lot about a person or a government by the rules they establish, and even more by the rules they enforce. For example, you can learn a lot about who I am from the number one rule that I have established and strictly enforce in the Stanley household: "Thou shalt respect thy mama." There's a lot of freedom and grace in our home, but if one of my children violates that simple rule, things get more than a bit unpleasant. I let my children know that I *will* over-react. My discipline will not be fair, but it will be thorough! While I think it would be a good idea if every family made that rule a part of their domestic policy, that's not really my point. My point is that particular rule reveals something about my values. We protect best what we value most.

The same is true of God. His rules reflect his values. God's display of power over the Egyptians revealed his ability but very little of his nature. Egyptian mythology described gods that were capricious and cruel. What kind of deity was the God of Abraham? The people needed to know. **The Ten Commandments reassured the Israelites that their God was not only powerful but good.**

Three months after the Exodus, somewhere between Egypt and the promised land, God instructed Moses to meet him at the summit of Mount Sinai while the Israelites camped in the valley below. But before issuing the first rule, God said something that must have stunned as well as reassured Moses. He said, "I am the LORD your God . . ." (Exod. 20:2). Moses must have thought, *Wait! Did you say the Lord* your *God? Don't you mean the Lord* the *God?*

Today, we have more than three millennia of information (and misinformation) about God, but Moses and the Israelites knew almost nothing about him. All they knew was that God had freed them from slavery and that he intended to settle them in the promised land. The simple, seemingly insignificant pronoun *your* implied something profoundly new to Moses and the Israelites. Ancient cultures believed in territorial gods, imaginary deities that controlled specific regions. They worshipped gods that controlled various functions in nature, such as the sun, the moon, storms, birth, and death. But after so many years of oppression in Egypt, the idea of a personal God having a personal relationship with people had long faded from memory.

Your God implies a relationship, but the Israelites hadn't done anything to deserve or establish a relationship. As slaves on the run, they had nothing to offer. They didn't even know how to please him! Nevertheless, the phrase "your God" affirmed the fact that the Israelites already had a relationship with God. He said, in so many words, "You're in. You are my people."

Then the Lord took Moses down memory lane. "I am the LORD your God, who brought you out of Egypt, out of the land of slavery" (Exod. 20:2), which immediately called to mind the events of the Exodus. In the ten plagues, God made a mockery of the Egyptian mythical gods (Exod. 7:14–12:32). He protected his people from the plagues, including the final, devastating affliction in which the firstborn of every household died. The death angel "passed over" any house bearing the blood of a sacrificial lamb on its doorposts, blood that symbolized trust in God's mercy (Exod. 11:1–12:32). He miraculously parted the Red Sea, dramatically saving the Hebrews from the Egyptian army (Exod. 14:13–31). He gave them a pillar of cloud to follow by day and a pillar of fire by night (Exod. 13:21–22). He supernaturally provided water (Exod. 15:22–27) and food (Exod. 16:1–35) in the wilderness.

God's message to Moses could not have been any clearer: "You're not here to get in with me; you're already in. We're not here to establish a relationship; I did that three months ago by supernaturally delivering you from your captors." It was in the context of this preexisting relationship—a relationship that began more than six hundred years earlier with a promise to another undeserving man, Abraham, that God gave his people the Law. **God initiated a relationship with his people before he even told them what the rules were.**

Having established the relationship, having sealed the relationship, and having proven the security of the relationship, God *then* gave the people rules to live by. God knew something that every parent eventually discovers. Rules without a relationship lead to rebellion. God understands human nature. So he gave the Israelites rules after they shared a relationship.

A relationship begins and ends with trust. Furthermore, the level of trust indicates the strength of the relationship. No matter how much one person wants to connect with another, there can be no relationship without trust. So God's first commandment should come as no surprise: "You shall have no other gods before [or besides] me" and "You shall not make for yourself an idol" (Exod. 20:3–4).

The first commandment has to do with trusting God to meet every need. In this commandment God said to Israel, "I want to be your one and only God." Why did he need to say that? Because, for as long as anyone could remember, the Hebrews had been surrounded by people who worshipped many gods. Every culture of that time and every civilization that existed for the next two thousand years worshipped multiple deities. God didn't want the Israelites turning to multiple gods to meet multiple needs—storm gods to grow crops; fertility gods to produce offspring; gods of the sun, moon, planets, and stars to propel the seasons—he wanted to be their one, all-sufficient source of *everything* they needed. He said, "I want to be your one and only because—guess what?—I *am* the One and only. What's more important to me than your mere obedience is your believing that I *am* and that you trust in my character."

The second commandment sounds like a repeat of the first, but in reality it introduces a new idea: "You shall not make for yourself an idol in the form of anything in heaven above or on the earth beneath or in the waters below" (Exod. 20:4). This is not God's prohibition against worshipping other gods. This is God forbidding any attempt to erect any kind of monument, fashion any kind of statue, or create any kind of image that represents him. If the idea of a singular God was hard for ancient people to grasp, the notion of an invisible God made no sense at all. All pagan gods could be traced back to some aspect of nature, which ancient people depicted in the form of artwork—not merely for the sake of representation, but for actual worship. They bowed down before these images. They offered sacrifices, prayed, and chanted to these idols to gain their attention. They even fed and clothed these statues.

The Lord commanded his people to avoid making any representation of him for two important reasons. First, God is unrepresentable. He is utterly unique in every conceivable manner. Whatever humanity can create, he is bigger. Whatever wonder of nature we can observe, he is more majestic. Whatever power in the universe we can discover, he is unmatched. God didn't want his people attempting to make him manageable, something they could visit and then leave behind, something they could create and then neglect, something they could quantify and then ignore.

Second, God didn't want his people to become enslaved to inanimate objects when they had a living God ready and willing to set them free. Ironically, while Moses received these commandments from God on behalf of the nation, the Israelites compelled Aaron, their second-in-command, to fashion a golden calf. Not content with an invisible God who actually exists, they comforted themselves with a physical representation of an imaginary god. They set aside the God who miraculously delivered them from bondage to worship a god they could manage and manipulate to suit their own desires.

As Moses recalled the event and recorded the story, he allowed us to see these events from God's vantage point. In reading the story, we can see the events taking place simultaneously at the top and bottom of the mountain—God reaching out to the Israelites at the summit while the Israelites forsook him for a golden calf in the valley below. And from this perspective, we can appreciate the absurdity.

∼⌐

Having affirmed his exclusive claim on the Hebrews as his own people, the Lord then addressed the issue of religious authority. "You shall not misuse the name of the LORD your God" (Exod. 20:7).

In Hebrew, this most-sacred name is represented by four consonants, which correspond to the English letters Y-H-W-H. But because no one has spoken the name in many, many centuries, we don't even know for certain which vowels to insert. Even today, if you visit Jewish Web sites, they refer to the Lord as "G-d."

While honoring the Lord's name is very important, he didn't give this commandment to discourage people from calling out his name when they hit their thumb with a hammer. This commandment addresses a deeper concern. The clearest translation of the Hebrew in the third commandment is, "Do not misuse the name of the LORD." Or to paraphrase, *Do not attach God's name to something he hasn't attached it to himself, and do not leverage the name of God in order to accomplish your own agenda.* God was about to give the new nation of Israel a constitution of sorts, consisting of hundreds of laws and statutes, and he didn't want them to start looking for loopholes. God knew people would try to use his name to support their traditions as a means of nullifying or circumventing his law. By the time of Jesus, religious tradition allowed a person to dedicate all his or her worldly goods to God using a kind of estate-planning scheme. The person said, in essence, "God, all of my wealth and possessions are yours. I'm holding on to them, and they're yours when I die, but if you want to use them, just let me know." Then, when the aging parents of these schemers needed support, the children would say, "I would love to help you, Mom and Dad, but I have dedicated all of my wealth to God, and I'm storing it for him in case he needs it. You don't want to take what is the Lord's, do you?"

Using this clever ruse, they invoked the name of God to validate their schemes and support their greed. Jesus confronted them, saying, "You have a fine way of setting aside the commands of God in order to observe your own traditions! . . . Thus you nullify the word of God by your tradition that you have handed down. And you do many things like that" (Mark 7:9, 13).

This didn't stop with the religious authorities in Jerusalem. Religious authorities have been misusing the name of God to serve their own ends for centuries, often resulting in the most appalling atrocities in history. The crusades. The Inquisition. Ethnic cleansing. Terrorism. Abortion clinic bombings.

On a more personal scale, countless people can tell heartrending stories of how they were deeply wounded by a church or church leader. Almost everyone can remember a religious authority who used God's name to institute certain rules or traditions and then punished people for daring to oppose God's will. This is precisely what the Lord wanted to avoid. God instituted this commandment, like the first two, to safeguard the Hebrews' relationship with him.

~~⁀⁓

Whereas the first three commandments safeguard the divine relationship, the fourth celebrates it. "Remember the Sabbath day by keeping it holy" (Exod. 20:8). Or, thou shalt take a day off.

The Hebrew word *Sabbath* comes from the verb *to stop*. His people were to stop all work and devote an entire twenty-four-hour period to resting (Exod. 20:8). And to explain the reason for the Sabbath rest, Moses pointed back to the creation account. "For in six days the LORD made the heavens and the earth, the sea, and all that is in them, but he rested on the seventh day. Therefore the LORD blessed the Sabbath day and made it holy" (Exod. 20:11).

Moses' point was not that God felt exhausted on the seventh day and needed to put up his feet for a while. God rested—that is, stopped (same verb from which *Sabbath* is derived)—because he had completed all his work. He had provided everything humanity needed in six days.

God gave the Israelites the Sabbath day as a perpetual reminder of his provision. They were to rest in his faithful, abundant care. And to drive the point home, the Lord used the Israelites' circumstances.

After leaving Egypt, the people were not spiritually and organizationally ready to settle into the land as a nation. As it turned out, they would need an additional forty years of nation building! However, the people could only carry so much food and water. With supplies running low, the people began to complain against Moses, "You have brought us out into this wilderness to kill this whole assembly with hunger" (Exod. 16:3 NASB).

Then one morning they woke to find the ground outside their tents covered with a white, flaky substance. The people asked one another, "*Man hu?*" which is Hebrew for "What is it?" Consequently, they called this heaven-sent, daily bread *manna*. The Lord instructed them to gather only enough for one day's needs, but of course, many tried to store it overnight, only to find it rotten and crawling with worms the next morning.

The Lord used this daily bread lesson as a means of teaching his people to depend solely on him for their sustenance. He wanted to create a new culture of daily dependence and abiding trust that would remain a part of their national consciousness, even during times of great abundance in the promised land. This lesson would teach them that their provider is *God*, not the soil, or the economy, or a king, or foreign allies. Each day for more than forty years, the people depended on God's daily provision.

The Lord commanded the people to gather only enough manna for the current day, trusting him to provide again the next morning. However, he made one notable exception to the pattern of provision. On Friday, the people were to gather enough to provide for *two* days of meals, the sixth and seventh days of the week. On all other days, the manna rotted overnight. And it appeared on the ground every morning except Saturday, which the Lord had declared a Sabbath day.

The point of Exodus 20:11 is this: God will provide seven days of sustenance on six days of your effort. All provision comes from him, and there's nothing for you to do on the seventh day. So stop working for twenty-four hours. Enjoy this divine gift of R&R. Saturday's manna was a weekly reminder of God's provision. This system required nothing more of his people than trust in his faithfulness and goodness. He wanted—and still wants—his people to remember that while work is good and effort is encouraged, daily sustenance comes from him.

Again, the fourth commandment, like the first three, supports and reinforces the fact that Israel already had a relationship with God. It was just a matter of acknowledging their relationship and living in harmony with God's design for them. He called the Hebrews to live in complete dependence upon him and, as a result, to enjoy abundant living, spiritually and sometimes materially.

～⌒)

When the Lord brought the Hebrew people out of bondage to settle them in the promised land, he reaffirmed the relationship between his love and his law. He carefully orchestrated each event and every experience to teach the Israelites—and all of humanity through them—this fundamental truth: **God's law is never given to establish a relationship; God's law is given to confirm an existing relationship**.

Pause for a moment and let that sink in. The story of the Exodus and the Ten Commandments reflects something important about God's character. If we miss this, we will never understand the role of God's law in our relationship with him. Worse, if we misunderstand the purpose of God's law, his grace will forever remain a mystery.

The law of God is an expression of his grace. Think about your pet. Don't have a pet? Then think about my pet. We have a black Lab named Shadow. And we have an invisible fence that works about half the time. But that's beside the point. Now, based on what you know about pets, when do you suppose we took Shadow home and trained her to stay inside our yard? Before we bought her or after?

Exactly: after. Once she became ours, we taught her to live within certain boundaries. Imagine the absurdity of stealing her from her previous owner, rushing to our house, putting her in the backyard, and then making the argument that she was our dog *because* she was in our backyard. She didn't become our pet when we placed her inside our fence. She's inside our fence because she's our pet. She became our dog when we purchased her. Similarly, God doesn't throw fences around people to make them his. God gives rules of conduct to those who already belong to him.

Now, from time to time, Shadow figures out that the fence isn't working and she takes off to visit the adjoining neighborhood. When that happens, we usually get a call. And never once have I made the case that Shadow is not our dog because she is no longer in our yard, abiding by our rules. Nope. She's our dog whether she's in or out of the yard. Why? Because **obedience does not determine ownership**.

In the same way our family made a choice to purchase Shadow, God chose to purchase us from sin through the sacrifice of his Son. Okay, maybe not in exactly the same way. But you get my point. Shadow didn't earn her way into our possession (or into our backyard), and we don't earn our way into God's backyard either. He made a choice to make us his own by grace. We enter that relationship through faith, accepting his offer of forgiveness for our sins. And then and only then do we become accountable to his prescription for living.

In the next chapter we will look at the second half of the Ten Commandments. But as we do, keep in mind that those laws were not given to establish God's relationship with Israel. They were given to a nation already in relationship with him. And if you find yourself measuring your own behavior against these ancient yet relevant instructions for life, remember that what was true of Israel is true of you as well. These divinely inspired instructions stand not as a gateway into a relationship with God, but as a confirmation that you already belong to him.

CHAPTER 5

Ruled by Grace

The purpose of the Law was not to make us good,
but to keep us free.

Perhaps the best way to understand God's purpose for establishing rules is to go back to his very first rule. Remember that one? Seems a bit random to us now: "You must not eat from the tree of the knowledge of good and evil, for when you eat of it you will surely die" (Gen. 2:17).

That one commandment served as a daily reminder of God's authority over mankind. Obeying it kept things in their proper order and guaranteed that Adam and Eve would experience maximum freedom. As long as they didn't break that single rule, they were as free as two people could possibly be. What was true then is still true today: **maximum freedom is always found under the authority of God**.

As we saw in chapter 1, the introduction of sin changed everything. Sin made the world a dangerous place. The more dangerous the environment, the more rules that are required to keep people safe. There was no danger in the garden of Eden. So one rule sufficed. But no single rule could contain the ever-expanding scope of sin. As sin increased in the world, so the need for laws increased as well. But while the need for law has changed, the purpose of God's law has been the same from the beginning: to protect the freedom of those he loves.

But that's not intuitive.

When it comes to the law of God, we are all tempted to ask the same question Adam and Eve asked: *Is God trying to keep something good from me?* That question changes the subject from *obedience* to *trust*. Will I trust that God has my best interest in mind? Will I trust that his rules are for my good? This is why it is so important to remember that God issues commands to those who already belong to him. If God loves you, why would he strap you with commands in order to harm you? Why would God want to keep something good from you?

Every parent understands this tension. At every stage of parenting, there have been times when I've had to say no. And sometimes I do not have an adequate answer to the question that always follows a no. "Why?" I've never resorted to, "Because I said so." But on many occasions I've said, "I can't really explain why right now. I just need you to trust me."

Our heavenly Father finds himself in the same predicament with us. And as you read the history of the nation of Israel, it is clear that God found himself in that same predicament with them. Like us, when they trusted and obeyed, there was a benefit. But when they called it as they saw it, there were consequences.

When we trust and obey, it becomes clear that **the law of God is actually an expression of the grace of God**. And when we see it in that light, we understand the words of the psalmist when he says he actually "delighted" in God's law and "meditate[d]" on it both day and night (Ps. 1:2). When we see God's law the way he intended it, we understand that the grace of God and the law of God are not opposing concepts. There is no tension between the two. One is simply an expression of the other.

~~~

The final six commandments were given to preserve the nation's liberty in very specific ways. Specifically, God wanted them to maintain their freedom from tyranny and from the natural consequences of sin. While living in Egypt, the Hebrew people knew only the rule of pharaohs. The pharaoh's word was law. Justice was as he saw fit. Might determined what was right. When a new pharaoh took his place, the rules were subject to change—sometimes dramatically. The only real absolute was the word of the pharaoh.

That was how law and government worked in ancient times. People were subject to the whims of powerful men. And when men establish law, they inevitably view themselves as above the law. I know this from personal experience. In the Stanley household, we obey the rules God established. We don't steal. We don't lie. We treat others with respect. But we also have a few rules that originated with me. For example, I made the following rule: "Thou shalt not stand in front of the open refrigerator and drink directly from the milk carton." Since that's my law, I feel empowered to break it whenever I want to. I don't lie awake at night wrestling with my conscience or fretting over my decision to drink from the milk carton. I feel no accountability to God for breaking that law, because he didn't establish it. I did. And the same holds true for anyone who establishes rules, whether for a household, a club, a company, a church, or a nation.

By giving Israel the Law, while not establishing a king, God made it possible for the Hebrew people to live under the rule of law, rather than the rule of man. Under God's newly established code of law, everyone received equal treatment. Unlike the laws of other ancient nations, this revolutionary system of justice elevated the status of women, children, foreigners, and even servants. Everyone enjoyed divinely appointed rights, regardless of power, social ranking, status, or wealth, because everyone answered to God as king. No longer would the people of Israel find themselves subject to the ever-shifting standards of a capricious pharaoh.

God's intent was for Israel to remain a theocracy. He wanted the surrounding pagan nations to watch with wonder as the Hebrew people built cities and roads, commanded armies, collected taxes, and maintained justice—all the normal functions of a nation—yet without a king. This would be a nation driven by love and submission to a divine Lawgiver. His intention was to establish a nation that loved his law because the people trusted its source. Eventually, Israel clamored for a king, and God granted their request (1 Sam. 8:19–21). Even so, Israel's kings could not rule with capricious autonomy like other nations. Hebrew kings were bound by the constraints of divine law. They ruled the people, but they answered to God.

Commandments five through ten are highly relational in nature. They were given to teach the Israelites how to live peacefully with one another. Most of these are intuitive to us, but that's because we were raised in a culture that for the most part champions these values. And that is due in large part to the fact that the Ten Commandments were central in the thinking of our founders. But for Israel, a former nation of slaves, this was new territory. They had come from an environment in which there were practically no individual rights. An environment in which an individual could have been considered of lesser value than an animal. In Egypt, people were bought, sold, and traded as commodities. From that context we can begin to understand the dignity these simple laws brought to the men, women, and children of this new community.

The list begins with a surprising commandment. Before prohibiting murder, adultery, stealing, lying, and coveting, God instructed his people to "Honor your father and your mother." And with this commandment in particular, he included a sobering rationale: ". . . so that you may live long in the land the LORD your God is giving you" (Exod. 20:12). God regarded honoring parents as the key to a peaceful, orderly, stable society, saying, in effect, "Your nation will never be stronger than your families. How you treat your father and mother will influence how you treat your fellow citizens, which will directly impact the future welfare of your country."

The Hebrew term translated as *honor* most often applies to people of high standing, such as kings, priests, or foreign dignitaries. The command to honor parents, then, goes far beyond the minimal requirement of obeying them as children. The Lord expected his people to *revere* their parents, even as adults. God knew that people who revered their parents—however flawed they may have been—would struggle far less to obey the last five commandments. If you grow up honoring your parents, more than likely you will lean toward honoring the people around you as well. And the commandments that follow center on extending honor to others.

"You shall not murder" (Exod. 20:13). The Hebrews were to honor other people's bodies.

"You shall not commit adultery" (Exod. 20:14). God expected his people to honor one another's marriages.

"You shall not steal" (Exod. 20:15). He commanded them to honor others by respecting their ownership of property and possessions.

"You shall not give false testimony against your neighbor" (Exod. 20:16). God wanted them to honor the reputation of others.

"You shall not covet your neighbor's house. You shall not covet your neighbor's wife, or his manservant or maidservant, his ox or donkey, or anything that belongs to your neighbor" (Exod. 20:17). The Lord even prohibited dishonorable thinking! *To covet* means "to desire strongly." This goes beyond simply admiring something that belongs to someone else. Coveting occurs when desire for what someone else has begins to undermine contentment. Coveting also occurs when one person begins to resent another because of something he or she has. To covet is to desire something so strongly that it erodes the relationship.

In these six commandments, God said, simply, "To preserve your freedom, both personally and as a nation, honor one another."

In 1787, Benjamin Franklin—who, like Moses, was in the process of establishing a nation—restated this thought in a letter to a friend. He wrote, "Only a virtuous people are capable of freedom. As nations become corrupt and vicious, they have more need of masters."[1] He worried that the natural consequences of dishonoring others would tear apart the newly formed United States of America.

The value of the Ten Commandments for non-Jewish nations is found in the sobering reality that all governments rule by permission, subject to the sovereign power of an almighty Lawgiver, and they must answer to him. Therefore, the responsibility of each nation under God is not to create law but to *discover* law. God gave Israel specific laws to obey that would not be appropriate today. Many of those rules address issues no longer in existence. Instead, governments have a responsibility to discover the way God intended people to live in community so that our specific statutes may conform to his perfect pattern of human conduct. Only as governments discover and embrace God's law can they keep their nation safe while not trampling freedom.

As you consider the context into which these laws were given, it is easy to see they were not designed to keep Israel from something good. These laws were designed to protect the integrity of their relationships. In this way, these were laws that reflected God's grace toward his people. These laws did not stand in contrast to his grace. Like all of God's commandments, they were given to aid his people in their life of grace.

~~~

While the Lord gave his people the Ten Commandments and a complex body of laws to govern their new nation, he had something far greater in mind. The Hebrew people were his chosen instrument in a great plan to redeem the world from the eternal consequences of sin. The Hebrew descendants of Abraham were to be a priestly nation, a kingdom ruled by God, and the means by which other nations could come to know him. They were to become God's voice of truth in the world, teaching his ways and illustrating his truths through daily living (Deut. 6). And, ultimately, they would give the world a Savior, whom they called Messiah.

Beyond the practical, temporal purpose of forming a nation and guiding its people, God gave his law to humanity to accomplish an eternal purpose: to confront our sin and to demonstrate our need for a Savior. As the New Testament writers would later explain, **God didn't give the Law to make us good. He gave the Law to expose our sin**. He knew from the beginning that humanity would not and could not keep his law perfectly, even when reduced to ten simple rules of conduct. This is why he made provision within the Law for those who violate his commands. Within the Law we find instructions for restitution when an Israelite intentionally or unintentionally harmed a fellow citizen. We find specific punishments for certain infractions of the Law—again, intentional and unintentional infractions. The Law includes a detailed sacrificial system by which sinners could repent of their wrongdoing, find forgiveness, and restore their broken fellowship with God. Again, from the beginning God knew mankind wouldn't get it right every time. So the Law—along with the sacrificial system—exposed the sinful hearts of his people and stood as a constant reminder of their need for grace. Even here, we find the grace of God within the law of God. For the Law didn't simply condemn sin; it included instructions for making amends.

Each of the prescribed sacrifices became an object lesson for the worshipper. He had to offer his very best animal from the herd, one without blemish or defect. This reminded the Israelites that sin is costly and that someone always bears the consequences of sinful choices. It also taught him the concept of substitution—the idea that an ideal, blameless sacrifice could bear the penalty of sin for another. The sacrifice reassured the sinner that once a sacrifice had atoned for his sin, God would never hold it against him in the future. **The Law confronted humanity with both the seriousness of sin and the depth of God's grace.**

At the giving of the Law, an interesting thing happened that further illustrates the relationship of God's law and his grace. The Bible tells us that as Moses descended the mountain with God's law, nature responded violently. Understandably, this frightened the people of Israel. But notice their response: "When the people saw the thunder and lightning and heard the trumpet and saw the mountain in smoke, they trembled with fear. They stayed at a distance and said to Moses, 'Speak to us yourself and we will listen. But do not have God speak to us or we will die'" (Exod. 20:18–19).

"Where's the grace in that?" you ask. As unpleasant as that sounds, even God's terrifying glory was an expression of his grace. When the people trembled at the base of Mount Sinai, which rumbled and smoked and flashed in an awesome display of God's presence, Moses reassured them, "Do not be afraid. God has come to test you, so that the fear of God will be with you to keep you from sinning" (Exod. 20:20).

Even this terrifying display of power was for the welfare of his people. The Israelites had no history with the personal or national consequence of disobedience. Like a child, Israel was naive. There was no way for them to grasp what sin could do to their infant nation. There was no way for them to understand the danger of intermarrying with the pagan nations that surrounded them. They couldn't appreciate the compounding danger of financial debt. This was all new territory. So whereas God could not leverage their experience, he leveraged his overwhelming power to *scare* or *terrify* them into submission. Seem inappropriate to you? Not to me. When I was a kid, my dad put the fear of Dad in me on lots of occasions. I didn't fear the natural consequences of the forbidden activities. How could I? I was naive. But I sure as heck feared the paternal consequences. And that kept me out of a lot of trouble. Looking back, I would put that in the grace column.

～♫

By now you are probably making the connection. What was true of Israel is equally true for you and me. God's law, as restated in the New Testament, is an extension of his grace to us. His commandments don't stand in contrast to grace. They were given because of his grace. God has provided his law to enable us to maintain our freedom from sin and its consequences. Isn't it true that your greatest regrets would have been avoided if you had opted to obey rather than disobey God's law? Isn't it true that you would be *free* from certain painful and shameful memories?

Looking back, it is pretty easy to see that God's law is at the center of his grace. It's in the moment of temptation that this powerful truth slips away. In that moment, like Adam and Eve and Israel, we embrace the lie that God is trying to keep something good from us. That he is against rather than for us. If, in those moments, we could see those prohibitions as expressions of God's liberating and protective grace, perhaps we would resist less and submit more. And in doing so, we would allow grace to do its work in us. And we would remain free!

CHAPTER 6

Rescued by Grace

Grace is slow to judge and quick to deliver.

Ifirst heard the story of Israel conquering the city of Jericho as a child in Sunday school. War stories were always the most engaging, and this one was particularly engaging because we were taught a song that commemorated Israel's victory that day. Feel free to sing along:

> *Joshua fought the battle of Jericho,*
> *Jericho, Jericho.*
> *Joshua fought the battle of Jericho,*
> *And the walls came tumblin' down.*[1]

After story time and singing, we enjoyed a snack of fruit juice and those little yellow cookies with the hole in the middle.

Those are great memories, and I recall that particular Old Testament story with a sense of wonder. It taught me an important life lesson: I have nothing to fear when facing obstacles or intimidating enemies; a great and powerful God loves me and has promised to fight on my behalf! So imagine my reaction when, years later as an adult, I read the rest of the story:

> When the trumpets sounded, the people shouted, and at the sound of the trumpet, when the people gave a loud shout, the wall collapsed; so every man charged straight in, and they took the city. They devoted the city to the LORD and destroyed with the sword every living thing in it—men and women, young and old, cattle, sheep and donkeys. (Josh. 6:20–21)

Pause for a moment and imagine the sights, sounds, and smells of that day. The violent, bloody carnage that took place as the Israelite army killed every living thing in Jericho. For me, visions of Rwanda replay and I feel the same sick feeling I experienced during my visit to the Kigali Genocide Memorial Center. If you think about it for too long, you begin to feel a little like you've discovered a secret about God, a dark side people rarely see or try to pretend doesn't exist. It helps me appreciate why some people refuse to believe in the God of the Bible. I can understand why some reject the Old Testament God as a more primitive, inferior being compared to the tender, compassionate God of the New Testament.

The contrasting images of the Old Testament God and the New Testament version create a real and difficult tension. I won't insult you by trying to explain them away. The fact is, God is both terrifying *and* merciful. God hates evil *and* he loves people. **God punishes sin *and* he extends grace to sinners.** I don't subscribe to the belief that the God of the Old Testament and the God of the New Testament are two different deities. That's a convenient view, but it leaves me creating God in the image I'm comfortable with. And that's always a mistake. But to continue believing that they are one and the same . . . that leaves me, and a lot of other people, with some explaining to do. The carnage following the overthrow of Jericho demands such an explanation.

To get the complete picture, we need to examine the context for these disturbing events. So let's set aside our childhood memories and discard the jaded lens of the skeptic and examine this historical event as if for the first time.

Roughly 650 years before the battle of Jericho, God made an un-conditional covenant with Abraham, promising that he would become the father of a great nation, that he would receive God's special bless-ing, and that the Hebrew people descended from him would receive the land of Canaan as a perpetual inheritance. As we discussed in chapter 4, that's why we call Israel the promised land—because it was *promised* to Abraham by God. However, the Lord also predicted that the descendants of Abraham would become a great nation not in Canaan but in Egypt. These are God's words to Abraham as recorded in Genesis:

> "Know for certain that your descendants will be strangers in a country not their own, and they will be enslaved and mistreated four hundred years. But I will punish the nation they serve as slaves, and afterward they will come out with great possessions. You, how-ever, will go to your fathers in peace and be buried at a good old age." (15:13–15)

As we saw in the story of the Exodus, that's exactly what hap-pened. Four hundred thirty years later, a family of forty-five people had mushroomed into a nation of about three million, and "a new king, who did not know about Joseph, came to power in Egypt" (Exod. 1:8). Despite the resistance of this hostile regime, Moses led the Israelites out of Egypt to settle in the promised land, essentially bringing them back to their homeland.

In the meantime, of course, Abraham's former neighbors in Canaan multiplied, built cities, cultivated the land, and developed into a dozen or more distinct cultures. So when the Israelites stood on the borders of their promised land and prepared to occupy it as God had commanded, lo and behold, it was already occupied! Now this left the occupiers, the Canaanites as they are referred to in Genesis, with three options:

Option 1: Move out of the territory promised to Israel and settle somewhere else.

Option 2: Commit resources to fight and defeat the Israelites.

Option 3: Surrender to Israel and offer to be for them what Israel had been for Egypt, a nation of slaves.

The idea of an invasion offends our modern sensibilities. Pushing a group of people off their land sounds so wrong. After all, isn't that exactly what created our current Middle East crisis? Isn't that why the Arab world rails against Israel in our current generation? The answer to both questions is yes. But the Scriptures tell us that the landgrab described in the Old Testament had a twist.

Included in God's promise to Abraham regarding his family's eventual return to and possession of the promised land was the following comment: "The sin of the Amorites has not yet reached its full measure" (Gen. 15:16). Now, this is a really important verse; when you read this statement in context, the meaning is clear. While Israel was busy becoming a nation under the watchful eye of Pharaoh, the people groups living in the land promised to Israel were busy creating cultures that were pagan even by ancient standards. There was little or no regard for human life. Idol worship was rampant. Scripture and archaeology reveal civilizations steeped in some of the most shocking, abominable practices imaginable, including incest, bestiality, institutionalized sexual abuse of women, and child sacrifice (Lev. 18:24–28). These nations were so abhorrent that God decided it was best to blot them out completely. These were unredeemable cultures. Not the people, but the cultures.

The phrase "full measure" (Gen. 15:16) indicates that God was giving these groups ample time and opportunity to abandon their wicked ways. The fact that their sin at that point *had not yet* reached its full measure indicated that God was waiting to judge these nations; he would eventually hold them accountable for their deeds. And as you read the book of Joshua, it becomes apparent that God used Israel to judge and punish these pagan cultures.

But all of this brings up a thorny question: how would the Canaanites know that their pagan practices were offensive to God? How would they know they were *sinning*? And sinning against whom? What did they know about God? The answer to these questions is, we don't know. But we can make an educated and informed guess. The fact that God waited so long to judge the Canaanites for their sin (more than four hundred years) implies that they had probably been warned. In light of what we find elsewhere in the Old Testament, it's not a stretch to believe that God sent prophets to warn them of his impending judgment if they did not repent. God did this in other instances. Jonah was sent to Nineveh to call that non-Jewish nation to repentance. While we don't know if this was the case for the Canaanites, what we do know is that God was paying attention to what was happening in the promised land. And he was not encouraged.

As Israel crossed the Jordan River and entered Canaan, they came not only to conquer but to cleanse the land. With that in mind, God gave Israel strict instructions regarding their invasion. The Israelites were not to intermarry with the unbelieving people of the land. When Israel conquered a town, they were to destroy everything of value. They were not to enrich themselves on the spoils of war, as was the custom in ancient times. Certain cities were to be completely destroyed, never to be rebuilt or inhabited in the future.

For most of us, that sounds a bit extreme, and it is certainly uncharacteristic of the God we were introduced to as children. But remember, the effect of sin on the world was equally extreme. Everything in the world had been contaminated by sin. God was taking extreme measures to ensure that this nation he built from scratch got off to a good start.

The early years were foundational. But these would be the fragile years as well. Nothing could be left to chance. Like hovering parents intent on protecting a newborn from anything or anyone who may do their baby harm, so God hovered over the nation. And understandably so. This was to be a nation like no other. The resettling of Abraham's descendants in the promised land was a new and important chapter in God's story of redemption. Much was riding on the success of this relocation. So God took extreme measures to ensure that Israel was shielded from the influence of the surrounding cultures. For he knew that one day, from this fledgling nation, would come One through whom grace would be offered to all the cultures and kingdoms of the world.

Now, let's get back to our story.

Like any good military general, Joshua sent a couple of men to scout the terrain and survey the city's defenses. Posing as travelers, the men found room and board within the city walls with a prostitute named Rahab. Unfortunately, just before nightfall, the spies were spotted and word of their presence in Rahab's home reached the king of Jericho. The king ordered Rahab to turn in her Hebrew guests (Josh. 2:2–3). But she decided to hide the men instead. In doing so she risked her life. The king certainly would have had her executed for harboring spies. Ignoring the danger to herself, she lied when the city officials confronted her. "Yes, the men came to me, but I did not know where they had come from. At dusk, when it was time to close the city gate, the men left. I don't know which way they went. Go after them quickly. You may catch up with them" (Josh. 2:4–6).

Soon after the officials took off across the plain toward the Jordan River and the gates were shut behind them, Rahab returned to the roof, where she had hidden the spies under stalks of flax that had been laid out to dry. It was then that she explained why she had risked her own life to save theirs. Her speech not only reveals her motivation, but it also gives us a glimpse into the hearts of the Canaanites. She said,

> "I know that the LORD has given this land to you and that a great fear of you has fallen on us, so that all who live in this country are melting in fear because of you. We have heard how the LORD dried up the water of the Red Sea for you when you came out of Egypt, and what you did to Sihon and Og, the two kings of the Amorites east of the Jordan, whom you completely destroyed. When we heard of it, our hearts melted and everyone's courage failed because of you, for the LORD your God is God in heaven above and on the earth below." (Josh. 2:8–11)

Rahab affirmed her personal belief that the one and only true God had given the land of Canaan to the Israelites. Apparently, the promise given to Abraham 650 years earlier was commonly known among the Canaanites. As the sons of the covenant prepared to cross the Jordan River, the people living in the promised land understood the significance of their arrival. They had heard about the miracles of the Exodus and their military victories over other hostile Canaanites. Rahab described the mind-set of her countrymen when she said, "Everyone's courage failed because of you, for the LORD your God is God in heaven above and on the earth below" (Josh. 2:11).

In other words, many of the Canaanites acknowledged the reality of the Hebrews' God as the supreme ruler over the universe. They believed that he had given Canaan to the Israelites and that they were assembled on the east side of the Jordan, poised to claim their inheritance. Rahab, however, responded to these beliefs very differently than her countrymen. Whereas they prepared for war, she surrendered and asked for protection. Just before the Hebrew spies slipped into the darkness, she pleaded, "Now then, please swear to me by the LORD that you will show kindness to my family, because I have shown kindness to you. Give me a sure sign that you will spare the lives of my father and mother, my brothers and sisters, and all who belong to them, and that you will save us from death" (Josh. 2:12–13).

The two spies promised to spare her life and the lives of her family on the day of battle. Then, after the posse had been gone a sufficient time, the men climbed through a window and scaled down the city wall using a rope. During this time, the city was enclosed by two walls separated by roughly fifteen feet. Wooden beams spanning the gap became the floor joists for living quarters. Rahab occupied one of the upper floors, which had a window facing outward.

Before leaving, the men instructed Rahab to tie a scarlet cord in her window so the Israelite army would know which apartment to spare during the battle. Anyone gathered in her quarters on the fateful day would be saved.

The similarities between this arrangement and Passover are too obvious to miss. On the night of the final plague in Egypt, when the death angel moved through the land, taking the lives of firstborn males, any house with lamb's blood smeared on the door frame was spared, or passed over. As God extended his grace to the Egyptians, Israel's tormentors, so he extended his grace to a pagan prostitute who knew nothing other than the name of Israel's God.

⁓

By the time Joshua succeeded Moses as the nation's leader, he had become a seasoned general. When the time came to attack Jericho, he would have employed standard siege tactics, except the Lord intervened with an unusual plan. This is the part most of us remember from Sunday school. He told Joshua, "March around the city once with all the armed men. Do this for six days. Have seven priests carry trumpets of rams' horns in front of the ark. On the seventh day, march around the city seven times, with the priests blowing the trumpets" (Josh. 6:3–4).

Some have suggested that this may have been an attempt at psychological warfare. The men of Jericho feared the Israelites' God, so leading the procession with the ark of the covenant—the preeminent symbol of God's presence—would have been a stroke of genius. Moreover, the spies learned that the Canaanites were terrified and had lost their will to fight. A well-executed scare tactic might prompt the men to surrender the city voluntarily.

Interesting idea, except God planned to conquer the city supernaturally from the beginning. He instructed Joshua, "When you hear [the priests] sound a long blast on the trumpets, have all the people give a loud shout; then the wall of the city will collapse and the people will go up, every man straight in" (Josh. 6:5). So why bother with the parade? Why go to the trouble of a daily procession around the walls for six days? Why not march once, shout, and then flatten the walls on the first day? Could it be that the Lord gave the people of Jericho six nights to sleep on their decision to oppose his people? No doubt he would have honored ten thousand scarlet cords hanging from windows throughout the city. He would have been delighted to have the city officials open the gates of the city, abandon their false gods, abolish their degrading customs, and acknowledge Israel's God as the one true God.

During the six-day march, any number of individuals could have found refuge in Rahab's quarters. The spies didn't limit their protection to her family alone; they guaranteed the safety of anyone within her home. But six days passed, and no one other than Rahab and her family sought God's mercy.

On the seventh day, the Israelites marched around the city seven times. After the seventh cycle, the priests blew their trumpets, the people shouted, and the walls came down. There are many theories as to how this took place, and they are all interesting. Some say the reverberation of several hundred thousand voices brought the walls down. Others suggest the multitude of feet marching close to the walls undermined the foundation, causing them to topple. We don't know. And ultimately it doesn't matter. What we do know is that God received all the credit for Israel's victory that day. And if the nations of Canaan were afraid before, the fear factor was exponential after the victory at Jericho.

When the walls collapsed, chaos ensued. The Israelite army converged on the city and followed the Lord's instructions to the letter. They killed every person within the city, slaughtered the livestock, destroyed the buildings, and set fire to anything that remained. Yet in the midst of all that carnage and chaos, God spared one household because of the faith of one Canaanite prostitute. At the end of the day, nothing of Jericho remained except for Rahab, her family, and their possessions. "Joshua said to the two men who had spied out the land,

'Go into the prostitute's house and bring her out and all who belong to her, in accordance with your oath to her'" (Josh. 6:22).

So the young men did exactly as Joshua had ordered. During the pandemonium of battle, as houses burned and swords clashed, a small Hebrew squad rescued Rahab, her father, mother, brothers, and "all who belonged to her." They escorted her entire family to safety.

> Then they burned the whole city and everything in it, but they put the silver and gold and the articles of bronze and iron into the treasury of the LORD's house. But Joshua spared Rahab the prostitute, with her family and all who belonged to her, because she hid the men Joshua had sent as spies to Jericho—and she lives among the Israelites to this day. (Josh. 6:24–25)

Don't rush by that last line. It's incredibly important. The storyteller, writing some years later but before Rahab's death, concluded his account with the remarkable epilogue, "And she lives among the Israelites to this day." A Canaanite prostitute, who otherwise would have been stoned under the law recently received through Moses, became an accepted member of the community, an adopted daughter of the covenant.

Her trust in God and her acceptance into the community entitled her to receive a portion of the land promised to Abraham's descendants. By surrendering her illegitimate claim to the land and by receiving God's gracious offer of mercy and forgiveness, Rahab became an adopted daughter in the family of God and an heir to Abraham's promise.

But the story doesn't end there! The gospel of Matthew reveals that Rahab didn't merely live on the outskirts of Israelite society, eating leftover milk and honey. Despite her sin-stained past, a young man named Salmon saw in Rahab a beautiful woman of faith, and he asked her family for her hand in marriage. Salmon and his bride, Rahab, gave birth to a son, whom they named Boaz. And Boaz, perhaps influenced by the remarkable courage and grace of his parents, married a dispossessed widow from Moab named Ruth. Boaz and Ruth later became the great-grandparents of none other than King David.

No longer a prostitute, clinging for survival to the lowest rung of Canaanite society, Rahab became a member of the Hebrew community. In time, she ceased to be known as Rahab the harlot. To them, she became Rahab, the wife of Salmon. Or Rahab, the mother of Boaz.

She eventually became a prominent figure in Hebrew history. She became the mother of kings, a progenitor of the greatest dynasty the world will ever know. Moreover, the Messiah, the King of kings, would be born from her lineage! Generations would look upon Rahab as one of the most fortunate women ever to find refuge in the mercy of God.

In the end, Rahab received far more than she originally surrendered. She received grace heaped upon grace and divine favor beyond her wildest imaginings.

∼◡

Rahab's story illustrates the wonder and beauty of God's grace with fairy-tale drama. But for all its uniqueness, her story is not so different from each of ours. Before Israel showed up outside the walls of Jericho, Rahab wore a label. Her neighbors, fellow citizens, customers, and even her parents knew her as Rahab the harlot. The people of Jericho may not have attached to the label the same things we do, but I have no doubt she felt the indignity of her occupation. Regardless of their culture or religion, women typically do not become prostitutes unless they are forced to. But when given the opportunity between dying with her pagan countrymen and surrendering to God, she chose the latter. As a result, she eventually received a new label: Rahab the mother of kings.

In some ways Rahab's story is our story. Each of us has a label. You may have had your label concealed for most of your life and prefer that it remain a secret. You deftly keep the people from your past separated from those who know you now. You avoid reminiscing too much because your memories and your old label cause you shame. In fact, your label may cause you to shy away from approaching God. Perhaps your label is the reason you hesitate to step foot inside church. If that's the case, consider this.

Isn't it interesting that when the Israelite spies offered to spare Rahab's life, they said nothing about her lifestyle? Abandoning her trade was not part of the deal. *Changing* her life wasn't discussed. She acknowledged Israel's God as *the* most powerful God and then hid his servants. That was it. Rahab's label was not an obstacle to God. And neither is yours! The reality and the embarrassment your label reflects is not an obstacle to God's grace. You, like Rahab, are invited as you are, label and all. You, like Israel, have been invited to join God in a relationship initiated by faith, not adherence to a set of rules.

This is the way of grace. And this is the way it has been from the beginning. Grace doesn't require people with embarrassing labels to shed those labels as a prerequisite. Grace is what empowers us to do so. Grace doesn't demand. Grace assists. When you look at Rahab's story within the context of God's patience with the nations inhabiting the promised land, the message is unmistakable: *grace is slow to judge and quick to deliver*.

This is true at a personal level as well. **When it comes to your labels, current or past, God is slow to judge and more than willing to deliver.** Not after you've freed yourself or distanced yourself from your embarrassing labels, but as part of the process. In fact, grace provides you with labels of its own: Forgiven. Accepted. Loved.

We don't know how long it took Rahab to completely shake her past. We don't know how long it was before she no longer viewed herself through the lens of her past behavior. My guess is that it was a process—a process that took time but that ended with her fully embracing her new life, her new identity, and her new standing with God. In the same way, it may take you some time before you can put away your label once and for all. But in the meantime, I want to encourage you to begin renewing your mind to the new labels that are yours through the grace of your heavenly Father.

To help you along that path, I've written a short prayer that is simply a way of verbalizing your recognition and acceptance of God's invitation to you. If this strikes a chord, I would encourage you to copy it down and read it over and over. Old labels don't fade fast. And sometimes it takes a while for new ones to stick as well.

Heavenly Father, I believe that your grace is more powerful than my label. I believe that Christ died to pay the penalty for the sin my label represents. I believe you are offering me a new label. Forgiven. Accepted. Loved. Today I declare that what you say about me is true. I am forgiven. I am accepted. I am loved. Teach me to live my life in accordance with who you say I am. Amen.

CHAPTER 7

Sustained by Grace

The grace of God has no load limits.

We all remember things our parents said growing up, especially those things they said over and over. A statement my dad was fond of repeating was something he paraphrased from a parable of Jesus: "To whom much is given, much is required" (Luke 12:48). He usually pulled that one out when he felt that I wasn't doing my best or wasn't fully leveraging an opportunity. And since that was often the case, I heard that one a lot.

I was definitely a "to whom much is given" person. I grew up in a great home with great parents. I've had more than my share of wonderful opportunities, including the opportunity to go to college and graduate school. If much is required from those to whom much is given, much will be required of me. And while I guess that's supposed to be motivating, at times it just feels like a lot of extra pressure.

So why am I bringing this up?

The fact that God extended his grace to Rahab by rescuing her and then including her in the lineage of Jesus is encouraging on one level. She was certainly undeserving of such an honor. Heck, she wasn't even Jewish. But you can't really hold the fact that she was a pagan prostitute against her. Rahab didn't really know any better. She was a pagan in a pagan culture doing what idol-worshipping pagans do. So while it's wonderful that God poured out his grace on her, you have to admit, she wasn't really a "to whom much is given"–type person.

You and me, on the other hand, we know better, don't we? We have Bibles.

We've been to church. I started a church! I've been a Christian since I was six. I should be way further down the path of spiritual maturity than I actually am. Unfortunately, becoming a Christian early in life means I've had time to make and then break more promises to God than the average person. I've broken more promises to God than most people make in a lifetime. If God's grace had a limit, I feel confident I would have used up my allotment a long time ago.

Fortunately for those of us who have been given much and are thus responsible for much, there is much grace. How much? More than we imagine. And no one in the Old Testament was more aware of that than the gentleman whose story will be the focus of this chapter. He was given everything a man could ask for. In his case, he knew without a doubt that everything he had came directly from the hand of God. Unlike Rahab, he knew better. He was without excuse. He knew the law of God. He had experienced the blessing of God. And most perplexing of all, he was given an exclusive promise by God. But in spite of all that, he turned his back on God. If ever there was someone whose behavior pushed him outside the reach of God's grace, it was this man. But in the end, he discovered, God's grace has no limits.

92

Our story begins twenty-five miles south of the ruins of Jericho in the town of Bethlehem. There, Rahab's great-grandson, Jesse, would be visited by a prophet. In those days a visit by a prophet signaled something of epic importance. The news was either really good or really bad. On this particular occasion the prophet was a bearer of good news. In fact, it was extraordinarily good news.

The prophet's name was Samuel. The news he delivered to Jesse was that God had selected one of Jesse's sons to be the next king of Israel. This must have struck Jesse as a bit strange, seeing as Israel already had a king. But he didn't argue; he just gathered all his sons together as Samuel instructed him to do. Well, he gathered seven of the eight. His youngest son, David, was apparently not king material. So he left him in the pasture, tending sheep.

When Samuel laid eyes on Jesse's oldest son, he thought for certain he had found God's choice for king. Eliab was tall. His handsome features would certainly attract followers and inspire men in battle. But alas, he was not God's choice. One by one, Samuel went down the row, briefly interviewing each young man, looking for a nudge from God. But the nudge never came.

At this point Samuel asked Jesse what I'm sure felt like an awkward question: "Are these all the sons you have?" But as it turned out, it was the right question to ask. "There is still the youngest," Jesse answered. "He is tending sheep." Samuel insisted David be brought in, and to everyone's surprise, he was the one.

The prophet anointed David's head with a few drops of olive oil in an informal yet significant ceremony. And the Scriptures tell us, "And from that day on the Spirit of the LORD came upon David in power" (1 Sam. 16:13). David then became known as "anointed one" or "the Lord's anointed." He was God's designated leader for the nation of Israel. But as soon as the impromptu coronation was completed, David rubbed the oil off his forehead and headed back out to the pasture to take care of his father's sheep. After all, everybody knew he wasn't a king. He was a shepherd.

David's story is a story of grace from start to finish. Why David? What had he done to deserve this honor? Nothing. Not a thing. And apparently his family agreed. They didn't even invite him to his own coronation. Besides, a new king should be the son of an old king. David wasn't even from the correct family. Yet God picked him. He picked him in spite of his family and in spite of his birth order.

~~~

Many years later, after David had secured the crown and defeated all his enemies, the Bible tells us that he got it in his head to build God a temple. Up until this time, the ark of the covenant, the wooden box that housed the original Law, resided in an elaborate tent. This was the epicenter of Jewish worship. For ancient Jews, the holy of holies within the tabernacle represented the presence of God. David called in the prophet Nathan and said, "Here I am, living in a palace of cedar, while the ark of God remains in a tent" (2 Sam. 7:2). The idea of a permanent place of worship struck Nathan as a good idea, and he encouraged David to follow through on his dream. But later that night, God interrupted Nathan's sleep and instructed him to tell David that though his idea was a good one, he was not the man for the job. The construction of the temple would be his son's responsibility. But on the heels of this disappointing news God made David a promise. An extraordinary promise. An unconditional promise with generational implications. God instructed Nathan as follows:

> "Now then, tell my servant David, 'This is what the LORD Almighty says: I took you from the pasture and from following the flock to be ruler over my people Israel. . . . Now I will make your

name great, like the names of the greatest men of the earth.'" (2 Sam. 7:8–9)

Chances are, you had heard of King David before picking up this book. That's exactly what that last line predicted. God told David that his name would be known beyond his generation. He continued,

"'The LORD declares to you that the LORD himself will establish a house for you: When your days are over and you rest with your fathers, I will raise up your offspring to succeed you, who will come from your own body, and I will establish his kingdom. He is the one who will build a house for my Name, and I will establish the throne of his kingdom forever. . . . My love will never be taken away from him, as I took it away from Saul, whom I removed from before you. Your house and your kingdom will endure forever before me; your throne will be established forever.'" (2 Sam. 7:11–16)

God promised David an enduring name, and it has endured. God promised David that his son would reign after him and build the temple; Solomon's temple is considered one of the wonders of the ancient world. And God promised David that his kingdom would endure *forever*. Forever. The repetitive use of *forever* was for emphasis. David's household would be the household of kings for as long as Israel had a king.

The Hebrew word translated "love" in the phrase "my love will never be taken away" is *chesed*, which appears nearly 250 times in the Old Testament to describe God's steadfast, unfailing, proactive, unmerited kindness. The Lord's *chesed* is grace. God's promise to David and his descendants was a promise rooted in his grace, not their performance. There were no *if you, then I* conditions attached to God's promise to David. This was an unconditional promise.

The Jews would later understand this series of promises to mean that the Jewish Messiah would come from the lineage of David. As it turned out, they were correct in their understanding. So it comes as no surprise that hundreds of years later, when Matthew sat down to write his version of the life of Jesus, he began with a genealogy. He knew that no one would take seriously a claim of Messiah without first establishing an indisputable family connection with David. In the same way, it was not a superfluous detail when the angels announced to the shepherds on the night of Jesus' birth, "Today in the town of *David* a Savior has been born to you; he is Christ the Lord" (Luke 2:11; emphasis added). The birth of Jesus was the ultimate fulfillment of the promise made to King David and his family. But that's just the beginning and the end of the story. The real story is what happened in the middle. It's the messy middle that makes this a story of grace.

At the very moment the Spirit of God descended on young David, the Spirit of God departed from King Saul (1 Sam. 16:14). But apparently nobody told Saul. So he continued to reign the best that he could. Eventually, and certainly providentially, David the shepherd boy gained national notoriety by killing Goliath. This led to a level of fame that eventually dwarfed that of King Saul. Just as David was growing accustomed to life in the royal household, he was warned by the king's son of a plot on his life—a plot designed by the king himself. So David fled. He took to the hills and caves of the southern Dead Sea wilderness of Judea. For the next fourteen years, David would be considered an outlaw and hunted as a fugitive.

Eventually he gathered a band of fellow fugitives and societal outcasts. Together they would live their lives on the run from a king who was determined to see his own son ascend the throne. At times David demonstrated extraordinary faith and integrity, acting as a man born to rule. Twice he spared Saul's life. On multiple occasions he placed himself in harm's way to defend his nation's borders. But at other times David would find himself overcome by the hopelessness of his plight. On these occasions fear would cloud his judgment.

In one tragic episode, David lied to the priests in the village of Nob in order to secure their help for the provisioning of his men. He claimed to be on an errand for King Saul. Consequently, the priests were eager to help with what he needed. But when Saul heard that the people of Nob had supplied his enemy with food, he ordered his general to slaughter everyone in the village. Men, women, children, priests, and animals were put to the sword (1 Sam. 22:18–19). The lone survivor, Abiathar, fled to David with news of the massacre. David was overcome with grief. He knew it was his fault. He had panicked. Taking responsibility for his failure, he said, "I am responsible for the death of your whole family." Then he swore to provide for Abiathar for the rest of his life.

In spite of this terrible lapse in judgment, David was still destined to become the king of Israel. God had willed it. He had willed it knowing that David would not always be worthy of this sacred trust. He had willed it knowing that a day would come when David would give him ample excuse to rescind his promise. But **that promise would stand. For it was not anchored by the behavior of the recipient, but by the grace of the One who had made the promise.**

After years of living like a bandit, David eventually ascended the throne of Israel. Both King Saul and his son Jonathan were killed in battle. The majority of the nation recognized David's right to the throne. After accepting the crown he transformed the loose alliance of Israel's tribes into a unified Hebrew nation. He secured the borders, conquering their pagan neighbors and reclaimed territory originally promised to Abraham. He strengthened Israel's economy and established it as a powerful presence in the region. It was during this season of success that God sent Nathan with the message that David's kingdom would be an enduring kingdom. But it was during this season as well that David made a series of decisions that would mar his reputation forever, decisions that made King Saul's indiscretions look like parking tickets by comparison. Anyone who knew the Law understood that David's behavior in the middle years of his reign disqualified him as king. And anyone who witnessed his actions firsthand would have expected God to annul his promise. But he didn't. God had not put any conditions on his promise to David. God didn't look for an out when David took improper advantage of the status God had granted him.

~~~~~~

The story of David and Bathsheba is so well known it hardly needs telling. So I'll be brief. Early one spring, as they did every year at that time, the Israelite army marched out to lay siege to an enemy city. But on this particular spring, for reasons we will never know, David chose to remain in Jerusalem. One evening, David strolled the rooftop of his palace, only to spy a young woman bathing. Curiosity got the best of him and he summoned a servant to ask about her identity. His servant's response was probably more than David had bargained for: "Isn't this Bathsheba, the daughter of Eliam, and the wife of Uriah?" (2 Sam. 11:3). It carried a subtle warning: *Your trusted friend, Eliam, and your much-celebrated lieutenant, Uriah, are risking their lives to advance your kingdom while you're back here leering at their daughter and wife.* But David ignored the disguised message and sent for Bathsheba to be brought to his chambers. We will never know how complicit Bathsheba was in this unfortunate affair. She may have been all too willing. Or she may have been afraid to say no to the king. All we know is that she spent the night with David and returned to her house the next morning.

A few weeks later, she sent a message to David, saying, "I am pregnant." Her husband, Uriah, had not been home in many weeks. So David had a mess on his hands. And he really only had two options: confess or conceal. Rather than face the consequences of his sin, David attempted to cover it up. He summoned Uriah from the battle on the pretext of getting a tactical report, hoping his time at home with Bathsheba would solve the problem. But the soldier elected to sleep in the palace among the servants instead. When David asked him why, Uriah replied, "The ark and Israel and Judah are staying in tents, and my master Joab and my lord's men are camped in the open fields. How could I go to my house to eat and drink and lie with my wife? As surely as you live, I will not do such a thing!" (2 Sam. 11:11). David insisted he spend another night in the city. This time he tried to get Uriah drunk and then send him home, but again the loyal soldier honored the sacrifice of his comrades, refusing to sleep with his wife.

At this point, it was all about damage control for David. So he did the unthinkable. David sent Uriah back to the siege with a sealed message for Joab, the commanding officer of the army. He ordered Joab to place Uriah in the forefront of the conflict and then pull back when the fighting became fierce. This was a death sentence for Uriah. But it was also a death sentence for the scores of warriors David knew would fight beside Uriah to the bloody end. This was a colossal abuse of power. This was murder.

Joab carried out his orders. Uriah was killed. Bathsheba played the part of the mourning wife. David played the part of the comforting friend. Then he brought her to the palace and married her. David succeeded in controlling the outcomes. But he broke just about every one of the Ten Commandments along the way. Whereas the people around him were powerless to address the evil done by their king, God was not. David's deeds were "evil in the sight of the Lord" (2 Sam. 11:27 NASB). This was an evil that could not be overlooked. As David was about to discover, **grace and discipline are not mutually exclusive. One does not preclude the other. Discipline is often an expression of grace.**

So one afternoon the prophet Nathan made an unexpected visit to the palace. The same prophet Nathan had on a previous visit assured David of God's everlasting favor. He confronted the king and the king broke. "I have sinned against the LORD," he declared (2 Sam. 12:13). Psalm 51 is believed to be David's official lament after being confronted by Nathan. Listen to the basis of David's appeal.

> *Have mercy on me, O God,*
> *according to your unfailing love;*
> *according to your great compassion*
> *blot out my transgressions.* (v. 1)

David understood that grounds for redemption and forgiveness were to be found exclusively in God's unfailing love. His only hope was grace. Later he declares, "You do not delight in sacrifice, or I would bring it; you do not take pleasure in burnt offerings" (v. 16).

David would not hide behind the ritual of animal sacrifice. He would not pretend that the blood of animals would make things right between God and him. There was nothing he could do. He was completely at God's mercy. David was genuinely repentant. Apparently, his heart was broken over his sin. And now he had no choice but to wait and see how God would respond.

The prophet Nathan was very direct with David that day. The consequences of David's abuse of royal power would reverberate for generations. Nathan declared,

> "Now, therefore, the sword will never depart from your house, because you despised me and took the wife of Uriah the Hittite to

be your own. This is what the LORD says: 'Out of your own household I am going to bring calamity on you. Before your very eyes I will take your wives and give them to one who is close to you, and he will lie with your wives in broad daylight. You did it in secret, but I will do this thing in broad daylight before all Israel.' (2 Sam. 12:10–12)

Then David said to Nathan, "I have sinned against the LORD" (v. 13).

Nathan's only bit of good news that day was that God would not require David's life. But he would take the life of the child born to him and Bathsheba (v. 14). As predicted, the child became sick and died. But that was just the beginning of David's troubles. In the ensuing years his family life became an endless series of public, humiliating scandals. His eldest son, Amnon, raped his own half sister, Tamar. For reasons we can only guess, David did nothing. The Bible tells us that "when King David heard of all these matters, he was very angry" (2 Sam. 13:21 NASB), but that's it. Emotion, but no action. No punishment. Nothing.

For two years, Tamar's full brother, Absalom, sheltered her, waiting for David to do right by her. But when it became clear that David would let the matter pass without justice, Absalom arranged to have Amnon murdered. Unsure as to how his father would respond to the murder of his firstborn and heir apparent, Absalom fled the country. David loved Absalom but did nothing to try and restore the relationship. Years later, when Absalom returned to Jerusalem, David refused to grant his son an audience. Two more years elapsed before Absalom forced a meeting through yet another round of reputation-damaging intrigue. After a tepid welcome from David and a less-than-ideal reconciliation, Absalom's resentment turned to sedition. He would get up early and position himself beside the road leading to David's court. When people came to plead their cases before the king, he would intervene, saying, "Look, your claims are valid and proper, but there is no representative of the king to hear you. . . . If only I were appointed judge in the land! Then everyone who has a complaint or case could come to me and I would see that he gets justice" (2 Sam. 15:3–4).

After four years of capitalizing on David's neglect of justice, Absalom led a conspiracy to eject David and install himself as king. He even rallied enough military support to overtake Jerusalem and put David to flight. He seized control of the palace and erected a tent on the rooftop, where he made a public display of sleeping with his father's concubines. He then began to hunt David, much like Saul had many years before. A civil war erupted. The borders were weakened. The enemies of Israel were emboldened. The entire episode ended with Absalom being hunted down and slaughtered in direct disregard to David's command to take his son alive.

David recognized his contribution to Absalom's rebellion and the carnage that followed. He had failed as a father. He had failed as God's agent of justice. He had refused to hold his own family accountable. He had placed himself and those closest to him above the Law. David understood that all of this was part of a much bigger picture, a picture framed by his own disobedience to the One who had given and promised him so much. In the end, David had only himself to blame. By every imaginable standard he had disqualified himself from the blessings and promises bestowed on him. God's grace had never been tested as it was with David. Other than Abraham, no one had been promised so much. And no one, including Abraham, had been blessed with so much wealth, power, and prestige.

Yet not even David's blatant disregard for God's extravagant blessings would stress God's grace to the point of breaking. **If grace had limits, David's behavior would have exposed them.** But

God did not withdraw his promise. He did not rescind his offer. No change of mind. Besides, this was never really about David. This was about God's unfailing love. This was and always had been a story of grace. Grace that has no limits. Grace that knows no boundaries. As the old hymn declares, "Grace that is greater than all our sin."[1] Even the sin of King David.

If we were writing the third act of David's life, I'm sure we would write it much differently than it actually turned out. Perhaps the biggest difference in the two versions would involve the role of Bathsheba. In our version she would probably be barren the rest of her life as punishment for betraying her first husband and participating in the cover-up of his murder. Or perhaps grief over the loss of her child would drive her to suicide or a life of seclusion. Poetic justice, perhaps. But nothing like that actually happened.

David and Bathsheba had a second child. A son. They named him Solomon. He followed his father as Israel's third king. As king, he led the nation into what is considered to be the golden age of Israel. He fulfilled his father's dream and built a temple. He is considered by many to be the wisest man who ever lived. And to top it all off, he is the author of three books of the Bible. Is that crazy? Apart from David's sin, Solomon would have never been born. One could argue that Solomon shouldn't have been born. But not only was he born; he was the son God chose to carry on the legacy promised to his father, David. That's grace. Undeserved, unmerited, unexpected, unexplainable, unbelievable grace. And so God became the ultimate Promise Keeper to one of history's greatest promise breakers.

While the details of our lives may overlap very little with David's, there is one thing we all have in common with him. We've all put God's grace to the test. We have broken his law. We've been irresponsible with his blessing. We've confessed a sin only to turn right around and repeat it. It's those occasions when I begin to wonder, *How many times? How many times can I expect God to forgive me for the same sin?* All of us in our own ways have wondered, *Where does grace end and retribution begin?* **If David's story is any indication, grace has no end.**

Hundreds of years later, this same sentiment would be repeated by a man who considered himself the "chief" among sinners (1 Tim. 1:15). In his letter to Christians in Rome, the apostle Paul wrote, "The law was added so that the trespass might increase. But where sin increased, *grace* increased all the more" (Rom. 5:20; emphasis added). Another translation says, "Where sin . . . abounded, grace . . . super-abounded" (AMP). That was certainly David's experience.

David's sin revealed the expanse of God's grace in such dramatic fashion that Matthew, a man who was no stranger to sin himself, could not resist referencing this dark chapter in the story of David as he compiled his genealogy of Jesus. In a list made up almost entirely of male ancestry, he reminds his audience of David's blunder: "Obed the father of Jesse, and Jesse the father of King David. David was the father of Solomon, whose mother had been Uriah's wife" (Matt. 1:5–6). One has to wonder why Matthew would pause to mention the one event in David's career that everybody wanted to forget. I believe he saw it as a pertinent detail to the story he was about to tell. Matthew, who had been eye to eye with grace personified, knew the grace that Jesus offered went far beyond the grace that religious leaders of his day offered. He saw in Jesus the grace David experienced. Grace that could absorb the full measure of sin. Grace that could absorb the sin of the world.

So regardless of what you've done, regardless of how far you've strayed, regardless of how long it's been since you addressed God directly, regardless of what you've been told, regardless of how you feel, grace awaits you. Grace that is far greater than all your sin!

CHAPTER 8

Puzzled by Grace

Grace is predictably unpredictable.

Perhaps the richest and most profound statement concerning God's grace is found in one of the strangest stories in the Bible—the story of Jonah. Skeptics have argued for centuries that this story could not have happened. No one can live for three days in the belly of a fish. And arguing that it was a whale, not a fish, is really not all that helpful. If this story is historical, then it required a miracle—actually, several miracles. Jesus referenced Jonah. Apparently he thought Jonah was a historical figure and that the events recorded in the book of Jonah actually happened. So that's my view. I always side with Jesus on debatable matters. Here's why: he rose from the dead. I'd like to do that someday. So I just go with Jesus' take on things, even when they are hard to take.

Having said all of that, if the story of Jonah is just too much for you to swallow, then I want to give you an out. Just think of this as a myth with a message. You've been inspired by fiction before. You've seen movies and read books that weren't historical but moved you to tears and made you want to be a better father, mother, boxer, gladiator, whatever. So put this in that category and follow along.

─◆───

As we finish our study of grace in the Old Testament and transition into the New Testament, the story and message of Jonah serve as a perfect hinge. This is not so much a story about a man who was swallowed by a fish as it is a story about a man wrestling with the competing implications of grace. Jonah was a man who understood what it meant to need grace. But at the same time, he found himself unwilling to extend grace to certain kinds of people. Mostly people who he thought didn't deserve it. But the problem, of course, is that nobody deserves it. If you deserve it, it isn't grace. But I'm jumping ahead.

Jonah lived in a tiny town near Nazareth around the eighth century BC during an unusual time of peace for Israel. Their two main enemies to the north—the Aramaeans and the Assyrians—had taken turns assaulting them over the past several decades, but both suddenly became preoccupied with other problems. So for about forty years, Israel was invasion-free. It was during this military lull that God called Jonah to complete a mission of mercy.

"'Go to the great city of Nineveh and preach against it, because its wickedness has come up before me.' But Jonah ran away from the LORD and headed for Tarshish. He went down to Joppa, where he found a ship bound for that port. After paying the fare, he went aboard and sailed for Tarshish to flee from the LORD (Jonah 1:1–3).

The city of Nineveh lay about five hundred miles northeast of where Jonah lived. Tarshish sat on the southern coast of Spain, more than 2,300 miles west, on the far end of the Mediterranean Sea. Jonah couldn't have chosen a destination any farther from Nineveh than the port of Tarshish. Jonah was not content to simply tell God no. He went in the opposite direction.

Interestingly, he didn't go somewhere familiar and he didn't choose an overland route. If you're running from God, why not go to a place you know to be safe and why choose the most hazardous mode of travel? Ships and navigation were primitive, to say the least. And the journey would have taken him through some of the most dangerous waters in the ancient world. But that's what people do when they run from God. They run to the strangest, most dangerous places and they make the most nonsensical decisions.

To be fair, I can appreciate why Jonah didn't want to go. Nineveh was the capital city of the Assyrian Empire, one of Israel's most vicious enemies. The Assyrians had turned cruelty into an art. They had perfected torture. They dismembered and disfigured people, skinned them alive, boiled them in oil, and impaled them on stakes. From Jonah's point of view, these people weren't worth saving. The last thing he wanted to do was be God's emissary of grace. They didn't deserve grace. They deserved judgment. So he ran. He went for the closest seaport and paid his passage to the farthest destination a ship could carry him. However, the rebellious prophet would soon learn a valuable lesson: **you can run from God, but you can't outrun him**.

～❍

Jonah loaded his possessions in the hold of the ship and breathed a deep sigh of relief as the coast of Israel disappeared below the horizon. But the voyage was barely underway before a sudden squall threatened to reduce the ship to splinters. The ship's crew began throwing supplies and cargo overboard to lighten the load while praying to their various gods.

Finally, the sailors decided the storm must be a supernatural punishment for someone onboard, so they cast lots, a form of divination, to discover which person had angered his deity. When all signs pointed to Jonah, the men confronted him. "Tell us, who is responsible for making all this trouble for us? What do you do? Where do you come from? What is your country? From what people are you?" (Jonah 1:8).

He answered plainly enough, "I am a Hebrew and I worship the LORD, the God of heaven, who made the sea and the land" (v. 9).

The sailors then asked a question completely consistent with their worldview. "What should we do to you to make the sea calm down for us?" (v. 11). As religious men, they believed that the gods sent natural disasters to punish people who displeased them. But Jonah knew the real reason for the storm. At that moment, he realized he could not outrun God. But rather than repent and call upon the Lord to forgive him and to save the ship, Jonah attempted suicide by sailor. He said, "Pick me up and throw me into the sea . . . and it will become calm. I know that it is my fault that this great storm has come upon you" (v. 12). He would rather die than go to Nineveh.

The pagan crew refused at first and attempted to row themselves to safety, but the Lord intensified the storm. Finally, unable to escape the consequences of Jonah's disobedience, they prayed to the God of Israel, asking his forgiveness, and threw the wayward prophet overboard as he had suggested. And for them, the story ends. The sea turned calm again. They undoubtedly returned to the original port of departure to reload and to tell their incredible story.

For Jonah, however, the story had only just begun. As he slipped beneath the waves, he was suddenly jolted to the realization that God hadn't given up on him just because he had given up on God. And that's probably a good thing for all of us to remember. But the broader context for all that was about to transpire was that even though Jonah had given up on the people of Nineveh, God had not. And so, "the LORD provided a great fish to swallow Jonah, and Jonah was inside the fish three days and three nights" (Jonah 1:17).

Three days and nights in the pitch-black, seaweed-filled belly of a fish is a long time. I don't know this for sure, but I don't think it took Jonah three days and nights to change his mind about going to Nineveh. I think he was bargaining with God about a second chance within the first few minutes. By the end of day one, I'm thinking he had promised God everything he could think of if God would get him the heck out of there. The reason I believe this to be the case is because my dad believed in spanking. In fact, he spanked me with his belt. And I would consistently begin my routine of repentance long before his leather made contact with my behind. As soon as he reached for his belt, I was apologizing, negotiating, sacrificing small animals. Whatever it took to avoid the pain, I was there. But because he was a good dad, he spanked me anyway.

So I don't think it took three days for Jonah to change his mind. I think it took three days for Jonah to learn his lesson. In the process Jonah learned something he would never forget: **God is thorough with his discipline**. Consequently, this was a lesson Jonah would not need to learn twice. Once would do. But that's not the only thing he learned from his three days under the sea.

~⁀）

After this ordeal was over, Jonah sat down and wrote out a version of the prayer he prayed while sloshing around in the stomach of the fish. I absolutely love the opening line:

In my distress I called to the Lord . . .

How many times have we done that, called on the Lord in our distress? Distress we created. Distress created by others. In Jonah's case it was distress of his own making.

In my distress I called to the Lord
and he answered me.
From the depths of the grave I called for help,
and you listened to my cry. (Jonah 2:2)

Why would God answer the prayers of someone who turned his or her back on him and then asked for help only after hitting bottom? A prayer of rededication doesn't carry much weight in the belly of a fish. What could be more self-serving? Yet even when the consequences of Jonah's decisions consumed him, and he was barely able to keep going, and he had no one to blame but himself, God heard his cry for help. Perhaps it was then that Jonah realized that **the purpose of God's discipline was not to pay him back but to bring him back**. In this way, the discipline of God was simply an unexpected extension of his grace. Even if it didn't feel like it at the time.

The prophet continued,

You hurled me into the deep,
into the very heart of the seas,
and the currents swirled about me;
all your waves and breakers
swept over me. (Jonah 2:3)

Yes, the sailors physically picked up Jonah and hurled him "into the deep," but God created the circumstances that made throwing him overboard necessary. The men merely became the instruments of God's strategy to discipline the prophet. But Jonah didn't resent the Lord for his actions. It's not uncommon for individuals who've spent a season running from God to later thank him for the difficult circumstances that brought them back. Disciplining grace is certainly not pleasant at the time. But it is appreciated later.

So while I don't think it took Jonah three days to repent, I do think he repented for three days. During that time it dawned on him that **to run from God is to run from grace**. As Jonah later wrote, "Those who cling to worthless idols forfeit the *grace* that could be theirs" (Jonah 2:8; emphasis added). Jonah realized that, like the pagan Ninevites, he had opted to serve his own selfish interests and in doing so *forfeited* or *lost* the full measure of God's grace.

When the time for Jonah's divinely appointed discipline was complete, "the LORD commanded the fish, and it vomited Jonah onto dry land" (Jonah 2:10). Can't imagine what that looked like. Or smelled like. Regardless, God offered Jonah a second chance to go to Nineveh. No surprise, he took it.

Now, while it's true that he obeyed the Lord and went to Nineveh, his heart wasn't in it. He still disagreed with God's decision to offer these violent, merciless enemies of Israel an opportunity to repent and thus avoid punishment. He wanted the Ninevites to pay for their crimes against his people. In his graceless way of thinking, they should get what they had coming. Jonah couldn't get past his prejudice. He was caught in the conflict of grace: it was something he was quick to ask for, but not something he was quick to dispense. Especially to the people of Nineveh. Yet he was still the man God chose to send. And resend.

Nineveh was a large city by ancient standards. Archaeologists have uncovered seven miles of wall enclosing eighteen hundred acres of space, enough room to accommodate 120,000 inhabitants within the walls and an unknown number living in the surrounding suburbs. According to Jonah it took him three full days to spread his message of repentance to the city. We can imagine Jonah walking the streets of Nineveh, perhaps wearing a sandwich board, and saying, "Forty more days and Nineveh will be overturned" (Jonah 3:4). He probably said it with all the passion and conviction of a man reading an eye chart, yet the people responded! They believed Jonah's message, declared a city-wide fast, put on sackcloth—the traditional symbol of mourning—and began calling on God to save them.

This took Jonah completely by surprise. He was a Jew carrying a message about a God the Ninevites did not worship. Why would his preaching have any impact at all? History reveals three events that may have prepared the city of Nineveh for repentance. First, they witnessed a total eclipse of the sun, a horrifying omen in ancient times. Second, a coalition of marauding tribes had been gaining momentum as they worked their way south toward Nineveh and had encamped about one hundred miles away. Third, the city had suffered two major plagues in five years that killed large numbers of people and continued to haunt their memories during this time. So by the time a prophet of their former enemy walked through their streets warning of impending doom, the people were primed for repentance.

~~◦

Now this would have been a great place to end the story. God was right, Jonah was wrong, the prophet obeyed, and he accomplished the mission with resounding success. But the story continues. When God saw the repentance of the Ninevites, he withheld the destruction he had threatened. But instead of breathing a sigh of relief, Jonah was furious. In a tantrum, he complained to God, "Is this not what I said when I was still at home? That is why I was so quick to flee to Tarshish" (Jonah 4:2).

Then Jonah made one of the most profound statements about God's grace recorded anywhere in the Scriptures. This is the kind of statement you would expect to find in the New Testament. It's certainly not something you would expect from the mouth of an Old Testament prophet—especially one with an attitude like Jonah's. If you still harbor doubts about the breadth of God's grace, pause and let this next statement wash over you. Here's Jonah's summary statement concerning God and his grace . . . in spite of how much it bothered him: "**I knew that you are a gracious and compassionate God, slow to anger and abounding in love, a God who relents from sending calamity**" (4:2).

Jonah reached back into the archives of his experience with God and concluded that God looks for opportunities to extend grace and compassion. It takes a long time to make him mad. He overflows with love. He often chooses not to give sinners what they deserve. And Jonah was fine with all of that as long as it was directed toward him and the nation of Israel. But the Ninevites? Are you kidding? Jonah was so distraught over God's grace toward Nineveh that he was ready to throw himself back into the sea (Jonah 4:1–4). He wanted justice. God insisted on mercy. He wanted judgment. God opted for compassion. Jonah's theology was impeccable, but his application was completely one-sided.

～⌒⌒♪

Shortly after telling God he would rather die than see the Ninevites saved, Jonah found a place east of the city, erected a temporary shelter, and waited to see what would happen. Would the city's repentance prove genuine, or was it merely a short-lived ploy to delay God's wrath? While he waited and watched, the Lord provided a fast-growing vine to shade the prophet from the hot sun. This made Jonah very happy. But the next day, God provided a worm to eat the shade plant. Then, to make matters worse, God sent a scorching east wind, known as a *sirocco*. These hot, zero-humidity winds typically blow out of the desert, carrying fine red dust and raising the temperature fifteen to twenty degrees within minutes. Unfortunately, Jonah had no way to take shelter from the elements. And again, he grumbled bitterly against his circumstances.

The story of Jonah ends abruptly, with Jonah entangled in a moral dilemma of sorts. A dilemma of grace. A dilemma much like the one Jesus would step into hundreds of years in the future. What follows are the final two verses of Jonah. Listen to God's question. Listen for God's *concern*.

> But the LORD said, "You have been *concerned* about this vine, though you did not tend it or make it grow. It sprang up overnight and died overnight. But Nineveh has more than a hundred and twenty thousand people who cannot tell their right hand from their left, and many cattle as well. Should I not be *concerned* about that great city?" (Jonah 4:10–11; emphasis added)

Kind of an odd ending, isn't it? But as we unpack this final exchange, you may find it to be more convicting than odd. God challenges Jonah with the focus of his concern. Essentially he says, "You've been concerned about—had compassion for—a gourd. A plant. A plant that brought you comfort. I, on the other hand, am concerned about a city full of people. People I created. Men and women who are like children in their understanding of me." To say that this reflected poorly on Jonah would be the understatement of understatements. On Jonah's list of concerns, the people of Nineveh ranked well below the welfare of a vine. While he was angry about the death of a plant that grew up overnight, Jonah cared nothing about the lives of the people in the city of Nineveh.

The plant represented God's grace to Jonah. The withholding of judgment represented God's grace to the people of Nineveh. Jonah was all about one, but not the other. He was grateful for God's multiple expressions of grace toward him but refused to celebrate God's grace toward the city. The moral of the story is pretty straightforward: **receiving grace is often easier than dispensing it**.

Jonah's sin was that his religion was really all about him. While he eventually surrendered to the will of God, he never surrendered to the purposes of God in the world. Although he was a descendant of Abraham, the man through whom the world would be blessed, Jonah could not see his way clear to extend grace beyond the bloodline of Israel. In spite of his esteemed role as prophet in Israel, the nation created to be a "light to the nations" (Isa. 42:6 NASB), he resisted the notion of extending God's grace to those outside the borders of his country. For whatever reason, Jonah could never embrace God's global message of grace.

But Jonah is not alone. When we open the pages of the New Testament, we discover that the sin of Jonah was the majority view in Israel. The early church was divided over this same issue. Truth be told, this conflict of grace has been an issue for Christians and for the church in every generation. So before we are too hard on Jonah, let's take a little inventory. Who are the Ninevites in your life? Who are the people to whom you have a hard time extending grace? Whose calamity do you secretly celebrate? Who do you secretly wish would get what you think they have coming to them? Let's start with some large groups. Rich people? Poor people? White people? Black people? Skinny people? Muslims?

Okay, let's narrow it down a bit. What about your sister-in-law?

Or your brother-in-law who divorced your sister and walked away from your niece or nephew? What about that ex-boss? Ex-partner? Ex-husband or ex-wife? I know what you are thinking. That's different. That's personal. While those kinds of situations are certainly personal, they really aren't all that different. Those are people who need God's grace, and someday God may assign you the task of extending grace in their direction. But that's between you and God. And if he decides you are the person for the job, I assure you, you will have a brand-new appreciation for our friend Jonah.

So grace has two sides: It is something to be received. It is something to be extended. The two are connected, but one is generally easier than the other. As we continue our study together, especially when we dive into the New Testament encounters with Jesus, I encourage you to keep your graceless relationships in mind. It may even be helpful to jot down some names or initials in the margin of this page. I'm not suggesting you do anything. I just want you to carry those faces with you into the second half of our discussion. Why? Because it could be that God wants to take you further than Jonah ever went. God may want to so overwhelm you with the reality of his grace toward you that you find it almost impossible not to extend that same grace to the graceless relationships that just came to mind. Grace can be irresistible in that way.

Selah

Storytellers understand the power of silence. Nothing arrests the attention of an audience quite like a well-timed dramatic pause, especially if the silence continues just a little longer than expected. By the design of heaven, a long, dramatic pause interrupted the story of God's grace.

After Jonah's successful mission to Nineveh, Israel's enemy responded to the Lord's gracious call for repentance. They heeded God's warning and, as promised, he withheld punishment. The Lord's covenant people, on the other hand, never fully repented. The nation of Israel, divided by civil war and plagued by idolatry, grew increasingly distant from him. After repeated warnings and severe chastisement, the nation God had ordained to be a light to the world entered its darkest period yet. He allowed a foreign nation to conquer the promised land and to carry the children of Israel into exile.

For seventy years, the Hebrew people lived in the land of the

Babylonians, a region formerly known as Ur of the Chaldeans (Gen. 11:31), the very place from which God had called Abraham. In a very real sense, the plan of God had returned to where it began. Moreover, from an earthly perspective, the grace of God appeared to have failed to accomplish anything. Pagan idolaters flooded into the promised land, and the people of God returned to servitude in a foreign country. Centuries of Hebrew history had come to nothing.

During these bleak years, the Lord assured his covenant people that despite the apparent victory of evil over good, his grace would prevail. He said,

> "When seventy years are completed for Babylon, I will come to you and fulfill my gracious promise to bring you back to this place. For I know the plans I have for you," declares the LORD, "plans to prosper you and not to harm you, plans to give you hope and a future. Then you will call upon me and come and pray to me, and I will listen to you. You will seek me and find me when you seek me with all your heart. I will be found by you," declares the LORD, "and will bring you back from captivity. I will gather you from all the nations and places where I have banished you," declares the LORD, "and will bring you back to the place from which I carried you into exile." (Jer. 29:10–14)

True to his promise, God returned a remnant of the original twelve tribes to the promised land, but nothing was ever quite the same. They reclaimed their inheritance with a sorrow-tinged joy. After seventy years in exile, the Jews who left Babylon—in a second exodus, as it were—returned to a home they had never seen. Like Abraham, they left everything familiar to sojourn in a land God would show them. For their new beginning, they rebuilt Jerusalem from rubble and reconstructed the Lord's temple with war-scarred stones. They struggled to keep hostile pagans at bay while maintaining a tenuous hold on their property. Meanwhile, the voice of the Lord grew quieter and came with less frequency. Eventually, his voice fell silent.

Four hundred years passed without a word. No authentic prophet of God spoke or wrote on his behalf. Like an unannounced intermission, the curtain of world events closed on the story of God's grace, and the stage went dark.

During this silence, the people of Israel struggled to survive, and the Lord met their faithfulness with miraculous affirmation of his love. For example, Judas the Hammer led the Jewish nation to victory over their invaders; after they'd successfully rid themselves of foreign rule, the Jews reclaimed their desecrated temple and relit the sacred lamps. Unfortunately, the priests found enough oil to keep them lit for only one day, whereas the process to consecrate oil took no fewer than eight. Trusting the Lord to provide, they began their work and, miraculously, the lamps remained lit all eight days. Today, nearly twenty-three hundred years later, Jews still celebrate the Feast of Dedication, or the Feast of Lights, more commonly known as Hanukkah.

Nevertheless, no prophet of God wrote a solitary prophetic word or uttered a single divine syllable. Another two hundred years passed in silence after the miracle of Hanukkah, during which hope for Israel dimmed with each passing year. Some abandoned their faith for something more tangible: religion fueled by human willpower. Others tightened their desperate grip on the promise of a Redeemer. Nevertheless, a remnant of believers trusted the character and power of their God, and they reminded one another of his promises.

In the garden of Eden, the Lord had warned Satan, "I will put enmity between you and the woman, and between your offspring and hers; he will crush your head, and you will strike his heel" (Gen. 3:15).

The Lord had promised Abraham, "All peoples on earth will be blessed through you" (Gen. 12:3).

The Lord had promised Judah, "The scepter will not depart from Judah, nor the ruler's staff from his descendants, until the coming of the one to whom it belongs, the one whom all nations will honor" (Gen. 49:10 NLT).

The Lord had promised the nation of Israel,

> "In the future, when you experience all these blessings and curses I have listed for you, and when you are living among the nations to which the LORD your God has exiled you, take to heart all these instructions. . . . The LORD your God will return you to the land that belonged to your ancestors, and you will possess that land again. Then he will make you even more prosperous and numerous than your ancestors!" (Deut. 30:1, 5 NLT)

The Lord had said to David, "Your house and your kingdom will endure forever before me; your throne will be established forever" (2 Sam. 7:16).

And in his last word before a four-hundred-year silence, the Lord promised a Savior for the ragtag, faithful remnant of Jews: "You, Bethlehem Ephrathah, though you are small among the clans of Judah, out of you will come for me one who will be ruler over Israel, whose origins are from of old, from ancient times" (Mic. 5:2).

Anticipation and doubt vied for the hearts of God's covenant people as deranged would-be messiahs emerged from the wilderness every couple of years. Each false Christ gathered a frenzied following only to lead them to slaughter, trying the faith of the faithful and justifying the cynicism of the corrupt. Then, with perfect timing and the grandeur of an act 3 overture, the grace of God shook the world. A piercing pinpoint of light attracted the attention of mystics on the far side of the Arabian Desert (Matt. 2:1–12). Somewhere in the pastures surrounding the backwater town of Bethlehem, an angelic host ripped the veil between heaven and earth to bring a stunning announcement: the Messiah is born (Luke 2:8–20)!

Just as the prophet Isaiah had foretold (Isa. 7:10–16), a baby brought new hope for Israel. Most had interpreted his oracle figuratively, yet the literal fulfillment of the prophet's vision lay in a makeshift cradle in the city of David. Born of a virgin. A descendant of David. A king worthy of Israel's throne. Immanuel, translated "God with us," carried more literal meaning than anyone could have imagined. In time, he would prove to all that in the birth of the Redeemer, God had not only come to rescue humanity from the death grip of sin; he had become one of us.

CHAPTER 9

Accepted by Grace

Grace is inviting to the unrighteous
and threatening to the self-righteous.

Being a pastor is both a blessing and a curse. Well, *curse* is probably too strong. Let's just say there's a downside. On the blessing side of the ledger, It's not uncommon for total strangers to pick up my tab at a restaurant. This doesn't happen all the time. But it happens frequently enough to make me glad I'm a man of the cloth. Unfortunately, nothing like that has ever happened at a car dealership or the Apple Store.

On the not-such-a-blessing side of the ledger, I make some people uncomfortable. When they find out what I do for a living, they become self-conscious. They apologize for swearing. Ladies button an extra button on their blouses. Kids take off their hats. Smokers put out their cigarettes. Or worse, they try to hide them. Not their cigarette pack, their lit cigarette.

I wish it wasn't this way. At times I feel like a surrogate conscience.

I walk into a room and immediately somebody starts feeling bad about himself. On several occasions an individual will discover I'm a pastor and will launch into an explanation as to why he or she hasn't been to church in a long time. I've had people start confessing sin. On the other end of the spectrum, people have immediately shut down the conversation once they discovered my occupation. They wanted nothing to do with me in spite of the fact that I'm really a pretty likable guy. My wife says so, anyway.

What bothers me most about all of this is that when I pick up the New Testament and read the accounts of Jesus' life, I discover that it was just the opposite with him. **People who were nothing like Jesus liked Jesus.** They weren't simply respectful; they liked him. They were comfortable around him. They invited him into their homes. They even invited their friends over to meet him—friends who, like themselves, were nothing like Jesus. As you read these accounts, something else becomes apparent: **Jesus liked people who were nothing like him.** He was as comfortable as they were. Maybe more so.

Over and over we find Jesus, God in a body, mixing it up with people who by their own admission were far from God. Yet there they are, face-to-face with righteousness personified. If that wasn't strange enough, on occasion Jesus would issue these non-law-abiding citizens an invitation. But not the invitation we may expect. His invitation was simple: "Follow me."

⁓

The apostle John experienced this firsthand. As one of Jesus' earliest followers, John watched him interact with people the religious system had discarded as unfit. He attended parties with Jesus in homes owned by the people his mother had warned him about. Following Jesus required John to step out of his religious comfort zone so many times that I'm sure he must have felt as if he were losing his religion alto-gether. Jesus was certainly like no rabbi he had ever seen or heard about. While extraordinarily devout himself, Jesus spent little time with the devout men of Israel. He was comfortable teaching in the synagogues as well as dining with notorious sinners.

To be sure, he was a paradox. But he was more than that. John concluded that he was in fact the Son of God, Savior of the world.

In the opening paragraph of his gospel, John summarizes all that would follow with these words:

> The Word became flesh and made his dwelling among us. We have seen his glory, the glory of the One and Only, who came from the Father, full of grace and truth. (John 1:14)

"Full of grace and truth." Jesus did not come to strike a balance between grace and truth. He brought the full measure of both. John had seen this firsthand. He had watched Jesus apply the perfect blend of grace and truth to each individual he encountered. And he was there the day Jesus extended his customary grace-filled invitation to the most unusual candidate imaginable: a tax collector named Levi.

No doubt, Levi loathed the man he had become. It was perhaps the only matter on which he and the men of the synagogue could agree. Despite his strong, Jewish name, the blood of Hebrews coursing through his veins, and centuries of Jewish culture oozing from every pore, Levi could not have felt more out of place in the promised land. His lower-middle-class upbringing had taught him to revere the piety of the Pharisees, but their hypocrisy turned his stomach. These out-wardly righteous men made a great show of religion, devoting the majority of their day to self-purifying rituals and public adherence to the law. Naturally, this left the Pharisees no time to earn a living, so they depended on donations from their working-class peers, receiving their hard-earned cash with one hand while shaking a finger at them with the other.

Then there were the Sadducees. It seemed to Levi that the aristocratic Sadducees understood their times better than anyone. They had come to terms with several unfortunate facts of life in Israel. Rome ruled Judea, and nothing short of a miracle would change that. No nation had successfully broken with Roman occupation in more than two centuries, so the choice was simple: destroy yourself against Caesar's ironclad fist, or go with the flow. The Sadducees openly chose the latter. But more than simply going with the flow, they had figured out how to turn their unfortunate situation into a source of revenue. The Sadducees never gave up hope of a free Israel, but they didn't see cooperation with Rome as anything but a realistic means of making the best of a bad situation. Rome wanted money, and the Jews wanted independence. The Sadducees satisfied the needs of both parties by presenting themselves as Jews while representing Rome's interests in political office. Unlike the Pharisees, they didn't hide their motives. Call it rationalization, but Levi found the Sadducees' open greed easier to accept than Pharisaic hypocrisy. So easy, in fact, he wanted to be like them. Consequently, he became a tax collector.

The Greek term for the office of tax collector was *telones*, a government post universally hated throughout the Roman Empire because of its inherent corruption. While Rome demanded a certain quota each month, the *telones* could use Roman authority to extort as much as he wanted. The actual tax went into Rome's coffers; the surplus made the tax collector very rich. To maximize his profit, he had to inspire enough fear to keep the money flowing yet not enough loathing to get himself killed.

For Jews in Israel, corrupt accounting was the least of the tax collector's sins. To become a *telones*, one had to purchase the office from another government official, which may require one to sell off property or mortgage one's estate. This sounds like a straightforward business decision to twenty-first-century Gentiles. After all, the sacrifice of real estate quickly turned a huge profit. But Jews drew their identities, in part, from owning a parcel of the promised land. To sell off a portion of the land promised to Abraham's descendants was to forfeit participation in God's covenant, not unlike Esau selling his birthright for a bowl of stew (Gen. 25:29–34). Therefore, Jews generally regarded tax collectors as traitors, men who had betrayed their people, their heritage, their temple, and their God. Like prostitutes who sell their bodies for money, tax collectors sold themselves to Rome. Even the Sadducees looked down on the office of *telones* as a loathsome yet necessary evil.

～～

Levi's parents took his name from the third son of Jacob, who fathered the Israelite tribe of Levi. During the Exodus, only the tribe of Levi remained faithful to God as the other eleven worshipped a golden calf (Exod. 32). As a reward for their faithfulness, God designated the descendants, or tribe, of Levi as priests. The role of priest would become an increasingly important role in Jewish religious tradition, especially with the construction of the temple under King Solomon. It was to the priests that the common Jew came when his sin demanded animal sacrifice. Priests were the attendants of God's house. It was a priest who entered the holy of holies once a year to make atonement for the sins of the people.

For any Jew to abandon his heritage to become a Roman tax collector was bad. For a member of the tribe of Levi to do so was beyond comprehension. Such a decision was considered traitorous. As a tax collector, he served as a financial go-between, serving an almost priestly role between the treasury of Rome and his Jewish kinsmen. In a culture that was supremely religious, where seemingly every month played host to a different festival or day of remembrance, his guilt must have followed him like a shadow. Every time he wrote his name, he was reminded of what he had become in contrast to who he had been born to be. But at the same time, the religious elite fed his contempt for religion with their work-around traditions and dumbed-down rules. He knew enough about what went on behind the scenes to know that many of the religious leaders were as corrupt as he was. True, he was a sinner. But he was not a hypocrite.

With all of that swirling around in the background, imagine Levi's surprise when the most prominent, dynamic rabbi in all of Galilee invited him to become one of his followers. For a man who experienced a conspicuous lack of invitations to events of religious significance, this must have come as a complete shock to his system. But Jesus' invitation was only the beginning of a series of new experiences that would eventually result in Levi becoming a different person. Even his name would change. Levi would eventually step into the pages of biblical history as Matthew, author of the first gospel—an account of Jesus' life with a distinctly Jewish flavor.

Matthew's first encounter with Jesus occurred on a day when the Lord and his disciples were visiting Capernaum. This busy fishing port sat on the northern shore of the Sea of Galilee and had become the center of Jewish religious life for the region. As Jesus taught, perhaps in the synagogue or a spacious home, four men went to extraordinary lengths to bring their paralyzed friend to Jesus for healing. The crowd watched with interest to see what Jesus would do. Among them were powerful

Jewish leaders and learned religious teachers. By this time there were rumors that perhaps Jesus was the long-awaited Messiah. Time would tell. As they watched, Jesus leaned down to this paralyzed young man and said something completely unexpected and somewhat irrelevant to the occasion: "Take heart, son; your sins are forgiven" (Matt. 9:2).

Now, as interesting as that may be, that was *not* the reason the men had labored to get their friend in front of Jesus. Those were not the words the paralyzed man and his friends had hoped to hear. They were looking for something more along the lines of "Be healed!" or "Paralysis, be gone!" A common priest could address the man's sins. It was the paralysis they wanted addressed.

But they weren't the only ones bothered by Jesus' pronouncement. The Jewish leaders in the crowd weren't very happy with his answer either. They considered his response blasphemy (Matt. 9:3). They believed that only God could forgive sins. So for Jesus to say, "Your sins are forgiven" was either a challenge to God's authority or an attempt to put himself on par with God. As they began to voice their outrage, Jesus brought all the drama to an abrupt end when he winked at the young man and said, "Get up, take your mat and go home" (Matt. 9:6). Well, actually, I don't know if Jesus winked at him or not. But I can't help but wonder if Jesus was kind of messing with him and his friends. He knew why they were there. And he knew who was looking over his shoulder. So he addressed the boy's immediate and ultimate issues with two remarkable statements. To everyone's amazement, Jesus said what only God can say and then he did what only God could do. So the boy stood up. Picked up his mat. And went home.

We don't know if Matthew saw this take place. Chances are, he was probably slaving away over a hot tax collector's booth. Regardless, he made sure to let us know that his own encounter with Jesus happened shortly after Jesus had said to a man, "Your sins are forgiven." He described his first personal encounter with Jesus this way: "As Jesus went on from there [*there* being the healing of the paralytic], he saw a man named Matthew sitting at the tax collector's booth" (Matt. 9:9).

At this point in the story, Matthew's readers would have grown apprehensive. The lowest of the low, a traitor to his people, a ceremonially unwashed moral failure looked up from his crooked ledger sheet to see the embodiment of righteousness coming his way. God in a body. What would the personification of holiness say to a man who had sold his soul to Rome for the right to steal from his countrymen?

And let's not forget that Jesus didn't travel alone. Trailing behind him were a number of his disciples, including James and John, who once wanted to call down fire from heaven to consume a town because they refused Jesus hospitality (Luke 9:54). We don't know when Simon the Zealot joined the group, but his name indicates he once associated with men who killed Roman sympathizers and other men like Matthew. The group also included Peter, who often engaged his mouth before his mind. What would these men say as they passed by Matthew's booth?

Before any could hurl an epithet and spit on the ground, Jesus said to the tax collector, "Follow me" (Matt. 9:9).

These were, by the way, the very same words Jesus used to invite James, John, Peter, and probably Simon as well (Matt. 4:18–22). But their invitations to follow Jesus made sense. They all came from devout Jewish families who worked and worshipped in Capernaum. They were hardworking, middle-class Jews who had remained loyal to their heritage and their God. No doubt they prayed for the coming of the Messiah and, in Simon's case, were willing to fight for the liberation of the nation. So imagine their reaction when Jesus invited a tax collector to become part of his inner circle. To become one of *them*. They must have gasped . . . or worse.

⌐◦

Many years later, after the resurrection of Jesus, Matthew was moved to write the story of how the Messiah came to forgive a sin-sick world and to redeem those considered by most to be unredeemable. In spite of his tenuous relationship with traditional Judaism, he told the story of Jesus from a decidedly Jewish viewpoint. Unlike the gospels of Mark or Luke, which plunge the reader into a fast-paced narrative, Matthew's gospel begins this way: "A record of the genealogy of Jesus Christ the son of David, the son of Abraham: Abraham was the father of Isaac, Isaac the father of Jacob, Jacob the father of Judah and his brothers, Judah the father of Perez and Zerah . . ." (Matt. 1:1–3).

Not the most fascinating way to begin a story. No modern author would dream of beginning a nonfiction work this way. Nevertheless, Matthew's genealogy of Jesus runs for sixteen verses, starting with Abraham and tracing his heritage through no fewer than forty generations to Joseph, the husband of Mary. But why? Why did Matthew begin his narrative this way?

Many have suggested Matthew's decision was based in part on the importance of establishing a solid pedigree. For a Jewish audience to even consider the possibility of Jesus being the Messiah, they needed to be convinced that he was related to the right people. In addition to all the usual suspects—Abraham, Isaac, and Jacob—Matthew knew he would need to connect Jesus to the kings of Israel. As we discussed earlier, the Anointed One had to come from the tribe of Judah and be a direct descendant of David. And so Matthew established Jesus' paternal bloodline through Joseph, his adoptive father.

Had Matthew stuck with the typical genealogical storyline, this explanation would suffice. But as we have already seen, he didn't. Matthew went out of his way to spice up his list with a couple of shady ladies and an editorial reference or two. Matthew was about to launch into an epic story of grace. A story that for many in his Jewish audience would seem disconnected from their Old Testament narrative. A story that would present God in sharp contrast to how the first-century religious leaders described him. He was about to suggest that God was concerned about Gentiles as well as Jews (Matt. 8:28–32), that he would forgive the most heinous sin. And that he would choose and use the most inappropriate people. Perhaps it was this last idea that created within Matthew his zeal for connecting his gospel to his Old Testament roots. For he was, in fact, one of those inappropriate people.

So he crafted this genealogy to foreshadow the purpose of God coming to earth in the person of Jesus the Christ. Matthew knew better than most that **the story of Jesus is the story of God drawing near to those who had been pulled away by sin and were subsequently pushed away by the self-righteous**. Matthew, therefore, presented a very unusual kind of genealogy, one that proved Jesus to be authentically Jewish, undeniably kingly, and—most important of all— born into a lineage of people who desperately needed the grace of God.

Providing a genealogy when telling the story of an important person is certainly not unprecedented. But Matthew's additional and, at times, inappropriate comments do make this unprecedented in at least one way. In ancient times, histories were written by men hired by generals, kings, emperors, and politicians. Specifically, they were hired to make their employers look good, and in some cases, to create a place in history for their employer even if a few details had to be exaggerated or fabricated. Consequently, these commissioned histories tend to have gaps. Victories and selfless acts of heroism get the full treatment with lots of colorful details. Military defeats and shameful political deeds barely get a mention, if anything is written at all. Children who make the family proud are always mentioned. Children who don't turn out so well? Sometimes they aren't mentioned at all. Genealogies were important to the famous in antiquity—especially to those who used their genealogy to establish their legitimacy to rule. So if there were to be any tampering with the bloodline, it would be for the purpose of cleaning it up, not cluttering it up

As Matthew went from begat to begat, it would have made sense for him to underscore the essential names on the list while possibly glossing over those that might detract from his story. But Matthew did just the opposite. As we've seen, he went out of his way to feature some of the most flawed individuals in Jesus' lineage. Instead of glossing over the embarrassing moments in Jesus' genealogy, he draws attention to them. What other historians would have omitted, Matthew highlights. For example: "Abraham was the father of Isaac, Isaac the father of Jacob, Jacob the father of Judah *and his brothers*, Judah the father of Perez and Zerah, *whose mother was Tamar*" (Matt. 1:1–3; emphasis added).

The phrase "and his brothers" contributed nothing to the genealogy if Matthew merely intended to trace the Messiah's bloodline. For any knowledgeable Jew, the phrase recalled the shameful treatment Joseph received at the hands of Judah and his brothers. It reminded the reader that of the eleven brothers, Joseph was the better man. Joseph became a savior to his people. Without Joseph, the family would have starved. Joseph was a man of grace and forgiveness. Judah, on the other hand, was a liar and an opportunist. Yet God chose to bring the Messiah into the world through the line of Judah. By adding that simple, unnecessary phrase, Matthew forced his audience to remember this irregularity in the story of Messiah.

Note also the inclusion of Tamar. Why a woman in a list of men? Better yet, why this particular woman? The reference to Tamar merely dredges up the embarrassing manner in which Perez and Zerah were conceived. As we discovered in chapter 2, had it not been for Tamar's deception, they would not have been conceived at all. God used this bizarre episode to accomplish his redemptive plan. The Messianic line continued through Perez, the son Judah fathered with Tamar.

Matthew continued his genealogy with a series of straightforward father-son mentions, but then he included the name of another woman: "Salmon the father of Boaz, *whose mother was Rahab*" (Matt. 1:5; emphasis added).

Why would he fail to mention Sarah or Rebekah and then go out of his way to bring up Rahab? She wasn't even Jewish. She was grafted into the family of Israel from a life of prostitution. But in Matthew's way of thinking, it was more important to include her name than the name of more honorable Hebrew women. By grace, God had reached into the pagan city of Jericho to save one repentant woman and her family. And by grace, he welcomed her into the family of Israel and made her the mother of kings.

But Matthew wasn't finished. "Boaz the father of Obed, *whose mother was Ruth*, Obed the father of Jesse, and Jesse the father of King David" (Matt. 1:5–6; emphasis added). By contrast, the story of Ruth is a wonderful story. Ruth's sacrificial love for her mother-in-law, Naomi, is a powerful example of grace. Especially when one considers the context of that relationship. But like Rahab, Ruth was not a Jew. Her parents were idol-worshipping Moabites. Ruth was a foreigner. Yet she was the great-grandmother of King David.

Again, Matthew seems to go out of his way to remind his audience that the Messiah's bloodline was tainted with the blood of Gentiles. But that was an essential part of Matthew's story. For as he would later explain, that blood was shed for people of all nations. For Gentiles as well as Jews.

But Matthew still wasn't finished. There were two more names that he believed deserved recognition: "David was the father of Solomon, *whose mother had been Uriah's wife*" (Matt. 1:6; emphasis added). The name of Solomon would have been sufficient to establish the kingly ancestry of Jesus and would have caused the mind of a knowledgeable Jewish reader to flash back momentarily, but Matthew wanted to be sure no one overlooked the scandalous conception of Solomon. He didn't write, "Solomon, the wisest man in the world," or "Solomon, whose mother was Bathsheba." Instead he added a detail that would emphasize the scandal around Solomon's birth.

No one would miss Matthew's point. Within the lineage of the Jewish Messiah was a handful of colorful characters. There were liars, swindlers, and lawbreakers. There was a murderer, a slave trader, an adulterer, and a prostitute. Perhaps—with a grin on his face—Matthew thought, *My kind of people*. At least they had been. And they were his kind of people right up until the day he met Jesus. **There was no point in hiding the fallen and flawed humanity of Jesus' ancestry. In many ways, that was the point of the story.** *They* were the point of the story he was about to tell. This was a message that first-century Jews needed to hear.

～～つ

When Jesus began his ministry, he found the nation of Israel divided over the issue of personal righteousness; that is, how a person gains and maintains good standing with God. One camp argued that a person could earn a right standing with God by keeping the law. To do this, however, they had to perfect the art of self-delusion. In addition to that, they had to dumb down certain commandments to bring them in alignment with the behaviors they had no intention of changing.

On the other end of the righteousness spectrum were those who refused to live in a perpetual state of denial regarding their personal unrighteousness. If the Law was the standard, they knew they would never be good enough to earn God's favor. So they simply kept their distance. Mutual contempt held the self-righteous and the self-condemned exiled in a perpetual dance of resentment. The self-righteous considered themselves better than the admittedly unrighteous. And the unrighteous felt judged by the so-called righteous, while at the same time seeing the hypocrisy between what they claimed to be and what they actually were.

By the time Jesus showed up, the temple had become the place where this division was most pronounced. Jesus illustrated the problem with a parable, most likely based on an actual event.

> Two men went up to the temple to pray, one a Pharisee and the other a tax collector. The Pharisee stood up and prayed about himself: "God, I thank you that I am not like other men—robbers, evildoers, adulterers—or even like this tax collector. I fast twice a week and give a tenth of all I get."
>
> But the tax collector stood at a distance. He would not even look up to heaven, but beat his breast and said, "God, have mercy on me, a sinner." (Luke 18:10–14)

That pretty much summed it up: one group who are not as good as they think they are, and another group who know they are not as good as they need to be. And there they were, together in the temple, *the* icon of God's desire to dwell with men and atone for their sin. The very design of the temple with its various gates and plazas stood as an invitation to sinners, both Jewish and non-Jewish. The sacrificial system, with all its blood and gore, was a daily reminder of man's inability to gain a right standing with God through right behavior. In the temple there was no room for self-righteousness and there was no need to cower behind one's sinfulness. Alas, it seemed everyone had missed the point. The self-righteous chased sinners away, and their own shame kept the sinners running.

And then Jesus showed up. He came to break the stalemate between self-deluded moralists and honest infidels. He came to shine a penetrating light of reality on the self-righteous and to offer those who were full of shame a way back. When Jesus met Levi, *he* certainly needed a way back. So when Jesus said, "Follow me," that's exactly what Levi did. He got up and followed. But Jesus didn't lead him to the temple. He invited himself over to Matthew's house. And oddly enough, Matthew didn't object. In fact, he got the word out to his friends that he was throwing an impromptu party and that everybody was invited.

Before long, Matthew's home was filled with fellow tax collectors, along with a broad assortment of less-than-righteous riffraff from all around the city. The Rahabs, Bathshebas, Judahs, and Davids of Capernaum all showed up for this unique celebration. They dined on Matthew's food and drank his wine, along with Jesus and his posse, who laughed and sang with Matthew's motley collection of religious and social outcasts. There under one roof was righteousness personified, celebrating right alongside unrighteousness on steroids. On that hot Middle Eastern afternoon, Matthew's home became a place of grace. For a brief time it served as a substitute temple of sorts. Here the righteous and the unrighteous had come together as they were, with no pretense for being anything other than who they knew themselves to be. *And Jesus was supremely comfortable.* Don't rush by that too quickly. **Jesus, God in a body, was not uncomfortable surrounded by those who most needed the bridge back to God that only grace could provide.**

But not everybody felt the way Jesus did. Standing on the outside of that sacred gathering were the religious icons of the community. The teachers of the Law. The Pharisees. The good people. Even if they were invited, they would never dream of entering a sinner's home. To do so would be to compromise their ceremonial purity. One touch from a sinner such as Matthew would require hours of washing. For this group, sin was a communicable disease. So it was always best to keep one's distance. As they huddled together, casting disparaging glances toward the party, they grumbled to some of Jesus' disciples, "Why does your teacher eat with the tax collectors and 'sinners'?" (Matt. 9:11).

Interesting question. We must assume they asked because they really did not understand how a man who claimed to be from God would get so close to those who were nothing like God. How was it that a man who was nothing like Matthew seemed to *like* Matthew? They had no category for this. And they had no patience for it either.

When Jesus heard about the objections of the religious elite gathered outside, he sent them a message: "It is not the healthy who need a doctor, but the sick" (Matt. 9:12). Jesus was playing to their categories for the moment. They assumed they were healthy. They assumed Matthew and his crew were sick. Jesus then quoted an Old Testament passage that would have been very familiar to the Pharisees. Matthew rendered the words of Jesus in Greek, but the Lord quoted the Hebrew text from Hosea 6:6. He said, "I desire mercy, not sacrifice." The word translated "mercy" is the Hebrew term we've run across before in our study: *chesed*. This was the term used to describe God's grace. "I desire grace, not sacrifice." His point? God prioritizes grace over sacrifice. Then Jesus offered them his one-sentence mission statement: "I have not come to call the righteous, but sinners" (Matt. 9:13).

Here, Jesus used the terms *righteous* and *sinners* with pointed sarcasm. It was his way of saying, "**I have not come to call those who think they are righteous, but those who know they are sinners**." If we could freeze that moment in time, we would be left with a startling and perhaps uncomfortable truth: grace is inviting to the unrighteous and threatening to the self-righteous.

Jesus' invitation for Matthew to become his follower, combined with his presence at Matthew's home, confirmed beyond all doubt that **grace is not earned; it is offered**. This was not a new idea. It was as old as the garden of Eden. But as would happen time and time again, the simple message of grace had been buried under a mountain of religious complexity—complexity created by men who sought to earn their righteousness rather than admit, and rest in, the truth that there is no righteousness apart from that which is given by grace.

In the years that followed, it would become clear to Matthew that Christ was God's grace personified. He would watch Jesus touch the untouchable and socialize with those who survived on the fringe of society. He would witness miracles performed on behalf of those who had done nothing to deserve them and could do nothing to repay him. Jesus would uphold the Law while embracing the law-breaker. He elevated the status of women and children. He paid his taxes, fed strangers, and loved his enemies.

As Matthew and his new friends traipsed along with Jesus from city to city, they would see only one thing that raised his ire: graceless religion. His conflict was not with Rome. It was always with the Pharisees, the Sadducees, and the teachers of the Law—those who knew best the stories of God's grace scattered throughout Israel's rich history. They were the stewards of Israel's story. It was their responsibility to keep the narrative of God's activity through Israel front and center in the minds of the people. But in this they had failed. On their watch there emerged a form of Judaism that was almost completely void of grace. It was this graceless religion that surfaced in Jesus a righteous anger that so set him at odds with the religious elite that they had him arrested, tried, and crucified. They leveraged the power of Rome, their sworn enemy, broke their own laws, and silenced the voice of grace.

But only for a moment.

Matthew had a ringside seat for all of this. And he was there when the news of an empty tomb was announced by Mary and her companions. Later he would see, touch, eat with, and worship a risen Jesus. And he would be given the privilege of penning a gospel. Not surprisingly, it's the gospel that contains the clearest proclamation of grace for the world at large. It is often referred to as the Great Commission. But perhaps it would be better entitled the *Grace* Commission: "Therefore go and make disciples of all nations" (Matt. 28:19).

All nations. This was a message for everybody. But perhaps the phrase Matthew connected with most was "make disciples." Literally, create followers. That's exactly what Jesus had done with him. He had made him a follower—a transformation that didn't begin with a command but with an invitation. It's an invitation that Matthew now understood was being extended to everyone: follow me.

～⌒

The tension between the self-righteous and the self-exiled did not end with the coming of Jesus. It is a tension that exists to this very day. So maybe this would be a good time to stop and ask yourself, "To which side of the aisle do I tend to lean?" If you had been invited to Matthew's party, would you have been a bit conflicted? Would your first inclination be to stand on the outside and wonder? Would you wonder why Jesus would fellowship with sinners before confronting their sin? Would you be concerned that by not addressing their sin Jesus was in some way condoning it?

Or would you lean the other way? Are there things about your current lifestyle or perhaps your past that would give you pause before walking into the presence of Jesus? Would a cloud of shame form overhead? Would you be tempted to stand outside in the hopes of catching a glimpse while avoiding eye contact? After all, you know. You know who you are and who you pretend to be. To bring all of that into the presence of pure righteousness? You would be crazy not to pause. Or would you?

Chances are, there's a little bit of both in all of us. We are judgmental of certain types of people or behaviors, and then we can turn around and put ourselves in time-out—self-inflicted exile from the presence of God. But in either case we step onto the well-worn path of graceless religion. Either way you choose you find yourself further from the grace of God. After all, the flip side of "I'm not worthy" is "But with enough time and effort I could be."

Here's what I think Matthew would tell us after watching Jesus: there's a third way. The way of grace. The way of grace is offered; it is not earned. It is offered to all people, regardless of who they are. So when you catch yourself bouncing back and forth between judging others and condemning yourself, pause. Pause and remember: you *can't* be good enough; you don't even have to be. That is the way of grace.

CHAPTER 10

Reborn by Grace

God's law reminds us of our need for God's grace.

P op quiz: What do all the following have in common?

- Klingons
- Philistines
- Cruella De Vil
- Sheriff of Nottingham
- Pharisees

Time's up.

As you probably guessed, these individuals or groups are all someone's nemesis, rival, or foe. *Star Trek* fans of all generations are familiar with the Klingons. If you grew up going to Sunday school, you know that the ancient Israelites were constantly doing battle with the Philistines. Disney's dogs with spots knew to steer clear of Cruella. The Sheriff of Nottingham was a constant thorn in Robin

Hood's side. And if you've read much of the New Testament, you know that just about everywhere Jesus went, the Pharisees were there, looking for an opportunity to discredit him with the populace.

If you look up the term *Pharisee* you will find at least two definitions. The first one will describe them as a first-century sect of Jewish religious leaders committed to a strict interpretation and observance of the Mosaic law. The second definition will be something along the lines of: a self-righteous, sanctimonious, or legalistic person. That being the case, most of us would rather be called a Klingon than a Pharisee.

In many respects, the reputation of the Pharisees is well deserved. They took adherence to the Mosaic law to unreasonable extremes. As if six hundred laws were not enough, they created additional lists of rituals to observe and behaviors to avoid to ensure that the existing laws weren't accidentally broken. They compiled a list of no fewer than thirty-nine activities one should not do on the Sabbath, ironically turning this day of rest into a labor-intensive day of religious observance. They also found great value in ceremonial washing. Here's a glimpse into the extreme measures this group took to avoid accidentally defiling themselves.

Water jars were kept ready to be used before every meal. The minimum amount of water to be used was a quarter of a log, defined as enough to fill one and a half eggshells. The water was first poured on both hands, with fingers pointing upward, and must run through the arm as far as the wrist. It must drop off from the wrist, for the water was now itself unclean, having touched the unclean hands, and, if it ran down the fingers again, it would render them unclean. The process was repeated with the hands held in the opposite direction, with the fingers pointing down; and then finally each hand was cleansed by being rubbed with the fist of the other. A very strict Jew would do all this, not only before a meal, but also between each of the courses of the meal.[1]

Despite the tediousness of their religious devotion, many Pharisees earnestly desired to please God and had earned the respect of their communities through kindness and generosity. Hillel, the most influential figure in Pharisaic history, is quoted in the Babylonian Talmud as saying, "That which is hateful to you, do not do to your fellow. That is the whole Torah; the rest is the explanation; go and learn."[2] These men were not unlike the most respected religious figures of our own day. They were considered the *good people*. These were the men considered most deserving of God's blessing in this life and the life to come. They were the model citizens of the kingdom of God.

Earning top marks among this unique group was a Pharisee named Nicodemus. If there were a category of "good enough," he was certainly in it. If righteousness could be earned, he had certainly earned it. If assurance of God's favor could be had in this life, Nicodemus had it locked down. Or so he thought. Then one day he met righteousness in a pair of sandals. And that's when things got a bit confusing

～⌒

Unlike Matthew the tax collector, Nicodemus the Pharisee loved the man he had become. Nicodemus had successfully risen through the ranks of Jewish politicians and clerics to become what Jesus called "the teacher of Israel" (John 3:10 NASB)—the *de facto* authority on all things religious. He wielded the power and influence of a Sadducee without losing the moral compass of a Pharisee. He influenced the aristocratic leadership of the temple while maintaining the esteem of the commoners.

For months, news had been trickling into Jerusalem from the rural province of Galilee about a remarkable new rabbi. His teaching style was riveting. He spoke with unusual authority. His insights into the kingdom of God were fresh and compelling. And perhaps most astonishing of all, it was rumored that he had the ability to heal diseases with a single touch. But there were disturbing reports as well: he claimed the authority to forgive sin, authority reserved for God alone. The religious authorities who were witness to these claims were outraged. But their complaints were viewed as petty when measured against his undeniable displays of power over disease and even nature. As crowds continued to swell and follow him from village to village, some were so bold as to utter the M word: *Messiah*. It was this last bit of rumor that most intrigued Nicodemus.

According to the gospel of John, Nicodemus was "a member of the Jewish ruling council" (3:1), a political body known as the Sanhedrin. For Israel, this was Parliament, the Supreme Court, and the Vatican all rolled into one. Seventy elder statesmen, guided by the high priest's right-hand man, represented the people before Rome and governed the people of Israel on behalf of Caesar. And they closely guarded their position of authority, not only because Caesar paid the ruling classes *very* well to keep the peace, but because everyone feared the wrath of Rome. Caesar and his governor allowed the Jews to worship their singular, invisible God and permitted them to govern their promised land according to their tradition, as long as everyone kept quiet and kept paying their taxes. Consequently, anyone claiming to be the Messiah—the king of the Jews—became a person of interest to the Sanhedrin.

The new miracle-working rabbi from Galilee had created quite a stir in the temple during the Passover feast. He not only shut down the business of merchants operating under the authority of the high priest, but he also claimed ownership of the temple itself, calling it "my Father's house" (John 2:16). The religious authorities challenged his claim, demanding a "miraculous sign" to prove his identity as the Messiah. Jesus merely brushed them aside to continue his ministry of healing, as if to say, "Just watch and you'll have all the proof you need." In truth, they weren't looking for validation of Jesus' claims. They were looking for ways to maintain their hold on the masses. The Sadducees and Pharisees jostled for political control, but they shared a similar vision for the future of Israel. Theirs would be a kingdom of God built upon shrewd politics and military might, led by a Messiah who affirmed their vision and supported their positions of power. Jesus didn't appear to fit that mold.

As much as they would have liked to, the Sanhedrin could neither dismiss nor discredit Jesus. After all, "many people saw the miraculous signs he was doing and believed in his name" (John 2:23). But it was too risky and too early to throw their support behind this wannabe Messiah. While they wallowed in indecision, the people were looking to them for direction. Is he or isn't he? The Sanhedrin had a real problem on their hands.

Not wanting to draw a conclusion based on hearsay, Nicodemus went to see Jesus to find out for himself. He went in private. He went at night. We are not told why he went at night. But since John includes this detail on purpose, it is probably safe to assume it had a purpose. It would have been a bit dangerous and confusing for Nicodemus to be seen visiting with Jesus. No doubt it would have surfaced questions among those who saw them together that Nicodemus was not ready or eager to answer. So he went at night.

Some have suggested that John deliberately drew attention to the nighttime setting to play upon the literary symbols of light and darkness. In the opening lines of his gospel account, he wrote of Jesus, "In him was life, and that life was the light of men. The light shines in the darkness, but the darkness has not understood it" (John 1:4–5). And as Nicodemus was about to discover, there was much that he did not understand.

～⌒）

Whether Nicodemus acted on his own or approached Jesus on behalf of the Sanhedrin, we cannot know for certain. But from what follows, we know he had a burning question—a question that was on the minds of many who had been exposed to the teachings of Jesus as well as those who had only heard through others: *Is he Messiah?*

Like every faithful Jew, Nicodemus lived with the silent hope that God's Anointed One would appear in his lifetime. It was a boyhood dream to witness the Messiah reclaim power and ascend the throne of Israel. He had grown up with stories of a warrior king who would someday inspire and lead the nation to overthrow Roman rule and restore the autonomy and security of God's promised land. Old Testament images of Israel as a dominant world power were stirred every time those stories were repeated in synagogues and homes.

Nicodemus and his peers expected the Messiah to be like David, only without the soap opera, or like Solomon, but without the harem. He dreamed in terms of military conquest and economic prosperity, so the elder statesman sought out Jesus to find out for himself. Was he the One?

～⌒）

While the question of Jesus' full identity remained a mystery, Nicodemus was certain of one thing: this miracle worker from Galilee had come from God and as such deserved the honor accorded a teacher. So he addressed Jesus as "Rabbi," a title of respect. "Rabbi," he said, "we know you are a teacher who has come from God. For no one could perform the miraculous signs you are doing if God were not with him" (John 3:2). This could have been flattery for the sake of diplomacy, but from what follows, that doesn't seem to be the case. Nicodemus was convinced there was something unique about Jesus.

What he did not anticipate was that Jesus knew the heart of every man. Jesus knew why Nicodemus had come before he asked his first question. The other thing Nicodemus was about to discover about Jesus was that he had an annoying habit of answering the question no one was asking but that needed to be asked. Jesus' insight into the heart of man enabled him to penetrate the error in a man's thinking and direct the conversation to the core of an individual's confusion.

So Nicodemus came with his questions surrounding Jesus' identity. But Jesus had another agenda. He would skip past the issue of Messiah and address an area of confusion in Nicodemus's view of God that had consequently confused his understanding of God's agenda for the nation and for the Messiah. Nicodemus's questions would be irrelevant because his presuppositions were all wrong. Yes, Jesus was the Messiah of God. But not the Messiah that Nicodemus was hoping and praying for. There would be no military campaign designed to liberate a few square miles of real estate. **This Messiah had something much larger in mind. He had come to liberate the entire world.**

As soon as Nicodemus completed his opening remarks, almost midsentence, Jesus interrupted and went to the heart of his confusion: "I tell you the truth, no one can see the kingdom of God unless he is born again" (John 3:3).

Huh?

Without warning, light was shining in the darkness. And it was blinding. Confusing. Threatening. Unnerving. As a diplomat, Nicodemus was prepared to be, well, diplomatic. As a diplomat, you slowly ramp up to the real issues. The important issues. But Jesus, in his entirely undiplomatic fashion, went straight to the heart of the matter. Nicodemus's view of the kingdom of God was all wrong. Consequently, his view of Messiah was skewed as well.

Nicodemus had been taught and, as a teacher himself, had taught that citizenship in the kingdom of God was the birthright of every descendant of Abraham. Jews were born into God's kingdom. For anyone else to join, they had to convert to Judaism. This involved a process of education in the Hebrew Scriptures and a ceremonial washing in water referred to as *baptism*. For men it was a bit more involved. They had to be circumcised. Only then could a Gentile become a participant in God's covenant with Abraham—and therefore a citizen of God's kingdom. These new converts were often referred to as "little children."

But all of that was beside the point. Nicodemus wasn't there to discuss entrance into God's kingdom. That had been a settled issue for centuries. The question at hand was whether Jesus was content to play the part of rabbi or if there was more to him than that. Was he Messiah? Nothing Jesus had just said fit into Nicodemus's carefully constructed worldview. As he understood the nature of God and religion, the formula was simple: Jews are in; Gentiles are out. After that it was all about keeping the Law. Lawkeepers merited God's blessing. Lawbreakers lived under the threat of judgment.

If Jesus had stopped with the word "born," everything would have made sense. Of course a person has to be born to enter the kingdom. If he had said "born to a Jewish father," that would have made sense as well. But "born *again*"? This was new. And it wasn't really what Nicodemus had come to talk about.

The phrase translated "again" uses a Greek term that can also be translated "from above" (John 3:31; 19:11). In order to enter the kingdom of heaven, one must be born from above. Born again, born from above—either way, Jesus was suggesting a second birth of some sort. He was implying that being a descendant of Abraham was not enough.

This wasn't just different; this smacked of blasphemy. But to go there would require Nicodemus to retract his opening statement: "We know that you are a teacher who has come from God. For no one could perform the signs you are doing if God were not with him" (John 3:2).

Nicodemus was stuck. He was confused. But he was also curious. So Nicodemus surrendered his agenda and leaned into Jesus' as best he could. "How can a man be born when he is old?" Nicodemus asked. "Surely he cannot enter a second time into his mother's womb to be born!" (John 3:4). No doubt Jesus grinned at the absurdity of the imagery. Perhaps they both did.

Rather than back down, Jesus pressed his point even further. "I tell you the truth, no one can enter the kingdom of God unless he is born of water and the Spirit. Flesh gives birth to flesh, but the Spirit gives birth to spirit" (vv. 5–6). The confused look on Nicodemus's face said it all. Jesus continued, "You should not be surprised at my saying, 'You must be born again'" (v. 7).

The meaning couldn't have been clearer. Jesus was telling him, "Nicodemus, you of all people should know that physical birth is not enough to gain someone access to God's kingdom. There's more to it than that. Something has to happen from above."

With all his education, with all his knowledge of the Jewish Scriptures, Nicodemus responded with astonishment: "How can these things be?" (v. 9 NASB). Perhaps what he was really saying was, "Now I see, but how could I have missed this for so long?"

Jesus continued, "I have spoken to you of earthly things and you do not believe; how then will you believe if I speak of heavenly things? No one has ever gone into heaven except the one who came from heaven—the Son of Man" (John 3:12–13).

Now things were getting completely out of control. Jesus was claiming to have come from heaven. Granted, Nicodemus had recognized that Jesus was "sent" from God. But literally came from heaven?

The implications were staggering. Either this man was a complete loon or—or perhaps he was who they had been waiting for. We have to give Nicodemus credit for remaining in the uncomfortable intensity of the light Jesus was shining on his ignorance and confusion. It would have been easy for a leader of his stature to take cover behind his education and pedigree. No one would have blamed him if he had chosen to scurry away before even more of his categories were scrambled by this itinerant preacher. Nicodemus had devoted his entire life to learning, teaching, and upholding a religious system that shaped his identity and gave his life purpose; yet he paused to consider the possibility that there was something he had missed.

Jesus, recognizing Nicodemus's sincerity, perhaps impressed by his willingness to remain engaged, looked for common ground in an Old Testament story he knew Nicodemus would recognize immediately. "Just as Moses lifted up the snake in the desert . . ." (John 3:14).

Finally! Something Nicodemus could relate to. Every Jew knew this story, which had transpired during Israel's migration from Egypt (Num. 21:6–9). The nation had wandered in the desert for forty years after leaving Egypt, not because they were lost but because they failed to trust God when it came time to possess the promised land. They had sent twelve spies on a reconnaissance mission, and ten returned with a negative report: they're too big and too many, and we're too small and too few (Num. 13:28–29). God disciplined Israel by causing them to wander around in the desert until that entire generation of doubters died off.

During their wandering years, the Israelites found themselves in an area inhabited by thousands of poisonous snakes. By the time they realized what was happening, it was too late to do anything about it. People were being bit by the hundreds, and many were falling by the wayside and dying. The Lord instructed Moses to craft a bronze snake and set it on a pole. Anyone who was bitten by a snake and looked at the bronze snake lived (Num. 21:9). It was an object lesson meant to teach the nation to look to God for their protection and provision.

But Jesus wasn't finished. "Just as Moses lifted up the snake in the desert, so the Son of Man must be lifted up, that everyone who believes in him may have eternal life" (John 3:14–15).

This was so much more than Nicodemus had bargained for. But at last he had his answer: Jesus was claiming to be the Anointed One sent from God. The Messiah. In his final statement, Jesus had positioned himself as the dispenser of eternal life. He believed himself to be the intermediary between God and man.

And the phrase "just as," meaning "in the same way," that was disturbing. A man lifted up on a pole was a man who had been sentenced to death. There was nothing in Nicodemus's theology that allowed for an executed Messiah. Perhaps he'd misunderstood. But that was not the most disturbing part. Jesus said "*everyone.*" Did he really mean *everyone*? Certainly he meant those who had been born into the lineage of Abraham, Isaac, and Jacob. But he'd said "everyone who believes."

The simplicity of this equation was more than Nicodemus could take in on this first encounter with Christ. **Jesus equated *belief* or *trust* with eternal life.** There was no mention of the Law, the temple, or the sacrificial system. The only possible connection was the inference that Jesus himself would be slain, and his execution would create some kind of bridge to eternal life. For everyone.

For someone raised to believe like Nicodemus, this must have sounded way too simple. If he understood correctly, Jesus was making eternal life—inclusion in God's kingdom—extraordinarily accessible. And as disturbing as that may have been, there had to be something liberating about it as well. For Jesus was not the only one who knew Nicodemus's heart. Nicodemus knew his heart as well. As hard as he tried to keep God's law perfectly, he knew he had failed. If eternal life was reserved for the truly good, even a man as devout as Nicodemus may not make the cut.

That's all we know of Nicodemus's first encounter with Jesus. There is no indication that he suddenly jettisoned several decades of religious belief in an instant. But neither did he run back into the darkness. He faced the intense, penetrating light of truth. And in time, his eyes adjusted. He saw what he had never seen before. He saw the necessity for the Messiah to die on behalf of his nation rather than lead them in a revolt against Rome. He saw that Israel needed to be saved from sin before any thought could be given to saving the nation from Roman occupation.

Time went by. Jesus' popularity among the people continued to escalate. The crowds continued to grow. But as his status among the masses increased, so did the anxiety among the Sanhedrin. Something had to be done. Siding with Jesus wasn't an option. But standing around while their influence over the populace slipped away was not an option either. The only *real* option left was to silence him.

After a failed attempt at having Jesus arrested, a group of Pharisees met with the Sanhedrin to discuss other approaches. Nicodemus was present. As the discussions became more and more sinister in tone, he found it impossible to sit by and say nothing. So at the risk of losing his credibility, he stood and challenged his peers with what I'm sure he felt was an appropriate question: "Does our law condemn anyone without first hearing him to find out what he is doing?" (John 7:51). They were stunned. Worse for them, they were cornered. Nicodemus was right. There had been no actual investigation. Only allegations. But not wanting to taint their opinions with facts, they simply changed the subject. They replied, "Are you from Galilee, too? Look into it, and you will find that a prophet does not come out of Galilee" (v. 52). On this point they were correct. But had they taken the time to look into it, they would have discovered that Jesus was not *from* Galilee. He was born in Bethlehem, the city of kings, the city of David. Seeing that they were getting nowhere, John tells us the group adjourned and went home (v. 53).

Nicodemus's initial encounter with Jesus left an impression. Something in him wanted Jesus to be right. Right about eternal life. Right about the kingdom of God. The duplicity of the Sanhedrin, the hypocrisy of the Pharisees, all of this left him wondering, hoping there was something more. Something better. Nicodemus had seen the light. And the light accentuated the darkness of the graceless religion he had grown up in. At last he understood the hypocrisy inherent to a system in which lawkeeping was essential to eternal life. Hypocrisy was unavoidable; if eternal life hung in the balance of personal behavior, then of course men would create ways around the law. It was no wonder so much effort went into redefining the rules and creating work-arounds for inconvenient prohibitions and requirements. But now his eyes had been opened and Nicodemus couldn't go back.

So we can only imagine Nicodemus's inner turmoil when he received word that Jesus had, in fact, been arrested and was being rushed through a series of mock trials in order to expedite his execution—an execution Nicodemus knew was a foregone conclusion before the trials even began. Perhaps he had been wrong to believe. But he knew with certainty that what was taking place in Pilate's hall was a greater wrong. But as it became increasingly clear that Jesus would not escape the cruelty of the mob or the injustice of Pilate's decree, something clicked with Nicodemus: this was what Jesus had predicted. This had been the plan all along.

Jesus' suffering and execution was a source of overwhelming disillusionment for the majority of his followers. His closest friends abandoned him in the end. And understandably so. With the disciples still looking for a Messiah who would restore Israel and expel the Romans, Jesus' crucifixion at the hands of Roman soldiers was the ultimate sign of defeat. They had been wrong; Jesus was not who they believed him to be.

But apparently Nicodemus didn't see it that way at all. What signaled a disappointing defeat for Peter, Andrew, James, and John indicated a new beginning for Nicodemus. This was exactly what Jesus had told him would happen. He knew! He knew because it was for this very reason that Jesus came. Not only did Jesus know he would be executed, but he even knew the form his execution would take. The event that did more to deflate the faith of Jesus' closest followers was the same event that brought everything together for Nicodemus. This Jesus was the suffering servant the prophet Isaiah had written of hundreds of years prior (Isa. 53:5)—the suffering servant whom the scholars of his day had failed to recognize as the coming Messiah. How could they all have missed it? Nicodemus knew the words by heart:

> *He was despised and rejected by others,*
> *a man of suffering, and familiar with pain.*
> *Like one from whom people hide their faces*
> *he was despised, and we held him in low esteem.*
> *Surely he took up our pain*
> *and bore our suffering,*
> *yet we considered him punished by God,*
> *stricken by him, and afflicted.* (Isa. 53:3–4 TNIV)

As the next line of Isaiah's prophecy formed in his mind, it must have taken his breath away:

But he was pierced for our transgressions,
he was crushed for our iniquities;
the punishment that brought us peace was on him,
and by his wounds we are healed. (v. 5 TNIV)

"Pierced for our transgressions." There it was. "Crushed for our iniquities." **Forgiveness and eternal life were not attained through the Law. Forgiveness required a payment.** Isaiah announced to the nation, to the world, that God would send a final sacrifice for sin. A sacrifice that would bring peace once and for all between God and man:

We all, like sheep, have gone astray,
each of us has turned to our own way;
and the Lord has laid on him
the iniquity of us all. (v. 6 TNIV)

Isaiah had foretold God's intention to place the sins of all mankind on the shoulders of Messiah. Now that day had come. Nicodemus's prayers had been answered. He had lived to see the redemption of Israel. But not in the way he anticipated. Not in a way anyone anticipated—but in the way God had intended all along:

Yet it was the Lord's will to crush him and cause him to suffer,
and though the Lord makes his life an offering for sin,
he will see his offspring and prolong his days,
and the will of the Lord will prosper in his hand. (Isa. 53:10)

In an instant, sacred literature that had confused Hebrew scholars for generations became penetratingly clear, as did the words of Jesus:

"The Son of Man must be lifted up, that everyone who believes may have eternal life in him" (John 3:14–15 TNIV).

Nicodemus stood in the crowd and watched as Jesus was lifted up. Perhaps he was the only one who understood the significance and sacredness of that moment. And as he watched the Messiah die, he believed. He was born from above. For the first time in his righteous life, he had assurance of a righteous standing with God.

Whatever concern Nicodemus had for his reputation and standing in the community vanished that afternoon. It didn't matter anymore. He broke ranks to join the tiny and discouraged band of Jesus' disciples. One of those disciples did not surface until after Jesus was crucified. Like Nicodemus, Joseph of Arimathea was a prominent figure in the community. Like Nicodemus, he had a lot to lose by publically identifying with Jesus. So he didn't. At least not until the end.

The Bible doesn't tell us what brought Joseph out of hiding, but the fate of Jesus' body probably had something to do with it. It was illegal to bury the body of someone who had been crucified. Crucifixion was designed as the ultimate public humiliation. So bodies were often left to rot for days after the victim had died. When the bodies were removed, they were put in the local dump. No formal burial or ceremony was allowed. This would have been the fate of Jesus had someone not intervened. On occasion, the family of the person crucified would petition officials for permission to take possession of the body and perform a proper burial. When an official request didn't work, a bribe sometimes would. So it wasn't completely unusual when Joseph of Arimathea approached Pilate for permission to take possession of Jesus' body. But he had to ask. Otherwise the body would have been taken down before Passover began, loaded on a wagon with the remains of those who had been crucified alongside him, and dumped outside the city.

But Joseph of Arimathea could not stand by and allow that to happen. So he chose to leverage his influence and his wealth and rescue the body. But in doing so, he blew his cover as a secret follower of the Savior. Here's how John describes it: "Later, Joseph of Arimathea asked Pilate for the body of Jesus. Now Joseph was a disciple of Jesus, but secretly because he feared the Jews. With Pilate's permission, he came and took the body away" (John 19:38).

But Joseph didn't act alone. "He was accompanied by Nicodemus, the man who earlier had visited Jesus at night. Nicodemus brought a mixture of myrrh and aloes, about seventy-five pounds. Taking Jesus' body, the two of them wrapped it, with the spices, in strips of linen. This was in accordance with Jewish burial customs" (John 19:39–40).

That's the last we read of Nicodemus. He had no way of knowing that his short encounter with Jesus would become one of the most popular stories in the New Testament. Of course, Nicodemus didn't know there would even be a New Testament. But there was something else Nicodemus had no way of knowing. Something of extraordinary significance.

His faith in and love for Jesus led him to do something Jesus' closest followers lacked the courage to do. His decision to take possession of and prepare the body of Jesus for burial provided first-century Christians with irrefutable proof of his resurrection.

The reason we believe Jesus actually died is because he was actually buried. Jesus wasn't dumped in a ditch. If someone who was crucified and removed from a cross after hanging there for only six hours showed back up in town after his body had been dumped, it would have been highly unusual but explainable. Obviously, he had survived. But if someone were taken down from a cross by people who would have looked carefully for signs of life, but having found none, prepared the body for burial according to Jewish customs, clearly, he was dead. If he wasn't dead before, he would have suffocated after being wrapped in layers of spiced and scented strips of cloth. Nicodemus's faith in Jesus led to the creation of the strongest evidence for his resurrection.

How fitting that the man Jesus told to be *born again* would pave the way for generations of people to have reason to believe that Jesus rose again. It was Jesus' resurrection that confirmed everything he taught regarding the significance of his approaching death. For Nicodemus, the resurrection would confirm those life-changing words spoken to him under cover of darkness: "The Son of Man must be lifted up, that everyone who believes may have eternal life in him" (John 3:14–15 TNIV).

～つ

We can't begin to imagine what it took for Nicodemus to admit he had been wrong his entire life regarding something as basic as what it took to gain admission to the kingdom of God. His assumption, up until his conversation with Jesus, made so much sense and was so widely accepted that there was no reason to doubt or consider an alternative. God gives good things to good people. Eternal life is a good thing. God must grant eternal life to people who are good. What could be more intuitive than that? That's the way it's always been. Why else would God have given Israel all those laws? Add to that the fact that Nicodemus was a good man. A really good man. A man everyone assumed was "in."

But after his encounter with the Savior, Nicodemus began to reconsider. In time, he was willing to let go of what he had always believed. He acknowledged that even he, one of the good guys, needed to be born from above. The law of God wasn't enough; he needed the grace of God.

Just as Jesus' words represented a radical departure for Nicodemus, perhaps they are a departure for you as well. If so, consider this simple idea that Isaiah predicted, Jesus taught, and Nicodemus discovered: **eternal life isn't a reward for good people; it's God's gift to forgiven people**. When Jesus was lifted up that afternoon on the hill of Golgotha, he was lifted up to carry the sin of the world. Your sin and mine. His death satisfied sin's requirements. Whatever you think you owe God, Jesus paid it. When Jesus said from the cross, "It is finished" (John 19:30), he meant it is really, truly finished. There is nothing for us to earn. There is only something to receive: forgiveness. And with forgiveness comes the promise of eternal life.

So the only question left for you to answer is: *have I ever received God's gift of eternal life by placing my faith in Christ's death as the full and final payment for my sin?* The only other option is to continue bartering for his acceptance through your goodness. And as Nicodemus finally understood, we just can't be good enough. God doesn't even expect us to be. So again, have you ever received God's gift of eternal life by placing your faith in Christ's death as the full and final payment for your sin?

If not, or if you aren't sure, I've included a prayer much like the one I prayed years ago. This prayer is just a way of expressing your faith in what Christ has done for you. As we leave the story of Nicodemus, I would encourage you to pause and consider whether you have been born from above through the grace of our Father.

Heavenly Father, I confess that as good as I've tried to be, I'm still not good enough to earn eternal life. I'm a sinner. I need more than a second chance—I need a Savior. I believe Jesus, your Son, came to this world to be my Savior. So right now I place all my trust in his death on the cross as the full payment for my sin. I'm no longer trusting in my goodness, my effort, my commitment, or my consistency. I'm trusting completely in Jesus. Thank you for forgiving me. Thank you for giving me the promise of eternal life. In Jesus' name I pray. Amen.

CHAPTER 11

Filled by Grace

Grace is God's response to the thirsty soul.

Q uestion: how much sand would someone have to consume in order to quench his thirst? I'll give you a minute to find your calculator.

I know. That's absurd. No one would try to quench his thirst with sand. Assuming he survived, it would only leave the person even more desperate for what he really needed: water (or at least something that has water in it).

Next question: how much stuff would an individual have to purchase and hoard in order to satisfy his need for approval? Doesn't really make much sense either, does it? Approval and things you can purchase are in two entirely different categories. You can have either without the other. But we both know people who have tried to leverage one for the other, don't we? You may have seen one in the mirror.

Last question: how many relationships would an individual need to pursue to satisfy his need for a relationship with God? No real connection there either, is there? But a lot of people have pursued that dead end.

God created mankind in relationship with himself. There's no indication that God had to introduce himself to anyone in the garden of Eden. Imagine that: "Hi Adam—it is Adam, is it not? I'm God, very nice to meet you. Oh, and is this your sister? Ha! Just kidding. You look way too young to be his wife."

Sorry.

Mankind was created in relationship with God. Sin, however, put a big kink in that relationship. Adam and Eve's sudden exit from the garden of Eden reflects the distance sin created between God and man. And that's a distance we've all felt at times. We've felt it when we were alone. Perhaps you've felt it when you were praying. Sometimes it's like an ache. Sometimes we experience it as a deep longing. Jesus described it as a thirst.

Now, as embarrassing as it is to admit, some of our approaches to quenching this thirst are really no different from his someone trying to quench their physical thirst with sand. And the results are not too different either. We just get thirstier. In my line of work, I encounter people every week who try to quench their thirst for God with anything and everything but God: relationships, food, sex, alcohol, work, achievement, approval, wealth, thrills, and perhaps the driest sand of all, religion. It's a problem as old as time and as universal as people. In John's gospel, he includes an account of Jesus stopping to help a thirsty woman connect the dots between her unquenchable thirst and a series of relationships that had left her even thirstier.

Jesus encountered this woman as he traveled from Judea, the southern region of Israel, to Galilee, the northern region. The territory known as Samaria lay between them. The shortest path between Judea and Galilee passed through the town of Sychar, where this woman lived, but Jews *never* took this route. No self-respecting Jew would allow his feet to touch the polluted soil of Samaria. The only accepted path from Judea to Galilee took a sharp turn east, *around* the territory. However, as John reflected on these events many years later, he wrote that Jesus "had to pass through Samaria" (John 4:4 NASB), which first-century readers would have found very intriguing. The Lord took the most convenient route in terms of geography, but it was extremely challenging culturally.

In 722 BC, King Sargon of the Assyrian Empire invaded the northern territories of Israel and carried out a unique plan to maintain control over his conquest. He dispersed much of the Jewish population throughout his empire and replaced them with Gentiles from other conquered territories. By shuffling people groups around and encouraging intermarriage, he virtually bred the Jewish race out of existence in his territories. Within a few generations after Sargon's conquest, no one in Samaria could claim pure Jewish blood.

Meanwhile, the southern region of Israel, known as Judah (or Judea, to the Romans), withstood Sargon's invasion. They later fell to Nebuchadnezzar, king of the Babylonians. He deported the Jews, but he didn't force them to intermarry. So when the Jews eventually returned to Judea, they started over as a pure race.

By the time of Jesus, several centuries later, Jews and Samaritans hated one another. Jews looked down on Samaritans as a polluted race. Samaritans despised Jews as elitist snobs. They were also divided by religious hostility. Jews worshipped in Jerusalem, on the original site of Solomon's temple. Samaritans established a rival temple on Mount Gerazim, the site of the original tabernacle. Neither recognized the legitimacy of the other's temple.

Nevertheless, Jesus "had to pass through Samaria." He had a divine appointment with a desperately thirsty woman.

The woman of Sychar had been married five times to five different men. That's unusual in our day and time, but it was extraordinarily unusual in that culture. Not only had she been married five times, but she lived with a man who was not her husband. The specific terms John uses suggest the man was not considered her husband because he was still someone else's. Her life bore the combined scars of tragic circumstances and foolish choices.

John doesn't reveal why she had five husbands. Perhaps all of them died. No shame in being a widow. But that kind of bad luck in ancient times would leave people wondering if she had been cursed by God. All her husbands may have left her for other women. Although blameless, imagine her overwhelming humiliation and debilitating sense of unworthiness. Some people barely survive one abandonment; what would five do to a soul?

We don't know if she went through five husbands because of decisions she made, or because five different men grew tired of her. We only know that life had been a struggle for this woman, and thanks to the small-town lifestyle of Sychar, where everyone knew everything about everyone else, public humiliation only added to her misery. Consequently, her bone-dry soul cried out for water.

Fortunately, a few days earlier and a few miles south, Jesus had planned his itinerary, and he had to pass through Samaria.

∼⌒

The noon sun beat down on the weary travelers as they approached a familiar landmark: Jacob's well. Jacob (aka Israel) had purchased this parcel of land and given it to his son Joseph as an inheritance (Gen. 33:19; Josh. 24:32). And when the Israelites departed Egypt, they fulfilled Joseph's dying wish by burying his bones on this plot of land. Jacob's well had been a place of refreshment and remembrance for more than a thousand years.

Jesus sat down by the well as his disciples headed into town to find food. On their way, they dutifully averted their eyes as a lone woman approached from the opposite direction, expertly balancing a water jar on her head. Traditionally, water was fetched in the cooler morning hours. Apparently, this woman preferred the afternoon heat to the company of the other women in town. A quick glance at the disciples' clothing confirmed they were Jews; other than that, she continued on her solitary mission as if they never existed.

As she approached the well, she saw another Jew sitting near the opening. Without a word, she placed the water jar on the ground, reached inside, and pulled out a generous length of rope. Just then, a voice took her by surprise.

"Will you give me a drink?"

Was this a joke? A Jewish man asking her to draw water for him with her Samaritan half-breed, sin-contaminated jug? Was he making fun? Was he lost? This was the last thing she expected. The only Jewish men she had encountered were prudish, snobbish, and racist. In their estimation, the only thing lower than a tax collector was a Samaritan. And the lowest form of Samaritan was a woman. Yet there sat a Jewish man, not only looking her in the eye and speaking to her, but indicating his willingness to drink from her vessel. Either he was on the brink of dying of thirst, or something else was going on. So she said the only thing she could think to say.

"You are a Jew and I am a Samaritan *woman*. How can you ask me for a drink?" (John 4:9; emphasis added).

Jesus answered, "If you knew the gift of God and who it is that asks you for a drink, you would have asked him and he would have given you living water" (v. 10).

Jesus used the expression "living water" playfully. Normally, the phrase referred to running spring water as opposed to stagnant cistern water. Jacob's well was both a storage cistern and a spring-fed water supply, depending upon the season.

The woman paused for a moment to search Jesus' eyes. Clearly, he meant something more than the obvious. Her quick wit found a clever reply. "Sir . . . you have nothing to draw with and the well is deep. Where can you get this living water?" (v. 11). In other words, "Either your words have deeper meaning, or your bucket doesn't go all the way down!"

She continued, "Are you greater than our father Jacob, who gave us the well and drank from it himself, as did also his sons and his flocks and herds?" (v. 12). She understood that Jesus offered something better than what she came to get for herself, but trust didn't come easily after so many betrayals and so much pain. Jacob's legacy—both his well and his religion—didn't quench her thirst for long, but it was familiar and it would be there tomorrow.

Jesus replied, "Everyone who drinks this water will be thirsty again, but whoever drinks the water I give him will never thirst. Indeed, the water I give him will become in him a spring of water welling up to eternal life" (vv. 13–14). John would reveal Jesus' definition for eternal life later on in his gospel: "this is eternal life: that they may know you, the only true God, and Jesus Christ, whom you have sent" (John 17:3).

The "water" Jesus offered was the very thing for which her soul was designed to thirst: a relationship with her Creator. *Eternal* life stood in sharp contrast to the life she had known. *Eternal* life was more than a woman like her could hope for. And perhaps that was what scared her most. For the first time in a long time, she felt a spark of hope. The thought that there may be something more than her current life reminded her of how thirsty she had become. So she had to ask.

"Sir," she said, "give me this water so that I won't get thirsty and have to keep coming here to draw water" (John 4:15).

What happened next is shocking. Cruel may be a better description. What is recorded next affirms my belief in the historicity of John's gospel. Why? Because no one would make this up. No one who was attempting to propagate a Jesus-myth would write this into the script. Honestly, I'm surprised this next section wasn't edited out!

Just as the woman opened herself to the possibility of hope, as she made herself more vulnerable than she had allowed for years, Jesus said, "Go, call your husband and come back" (v. 16). Her husband? She'd just asked for eternal life. She asked because Jesus encouraged her to ask. So why change the subject? But it was worse than that. Not only did he change the subject; he deliberately raked his fingernails across an open wound. Suddenly hope became pain, embarrassment, humiliation. Memories she had buried and reburied were forced to the surface. With them came the regret. How foolish to have hoped. "I have no husband," she replied (v. 17).

As she stuffed the rope back into the water jar and her protective shell began to close around her, Jesus touched her wound yet again. "You are right when you say you have no husband. The fact is, you have had five husbands, and the man you now have is not your husband. What you have just said is quite true" (v. 18).

As wrong and as uncomfortable as all of this feels to us two thousand years after the fact, let's not forget that Jesus knew the hearts of men. And women. He had come to this dusty well to give this woman eternal life. New life for an old life. Apparently, **Jesus knew that for the exchange to be complete, he had to dredge up all the old so that it could be replaced once and for all**.

As awkward as these moments must have been, she didn't walk away. Besides, how did he know? How did a Jewish stranger know so much about her? As threatening as his question had been, there was nothing threatening in those eyes. But either way, this conversation was over. She must have suppressed a sob as her fumbling hands continued to push the rope back into the water jar as if it were her dignity. Hoping a quick change of subject would buy her enough time to get away, she said, "Sir . . . I can see that you are a prophet. Our fathers worshiped on this mountain, but you Jews claim that the place where we must worship is in Jerusalem" (vv. 19–20). **It's always easier to talk about theology than our pain.**

Jesus allowed the woman her diversion. She needed this respite. Gently, he addressed her skewed perspective on worship and the importance of the temple in Jerusalem. He also revealed the future. The coming of Messiah would mark the beginning of a new era of worship. The dwelling of God would no longer be the magnificent temple in Jerusalem. His house would be the hearts of his worshippers.

With her rope haphazardly stuffed back into the jar, a patronizing smile crossed the woman's face as she said, "I know that Messiah is coming. When he comes, he will explain everything to us" (John 4:25). This was her first-century way of saying, "Bye, now! You have yourself a nice life."

But Jesus wasn't finished. He had come all this way for this moment. Now that her heart was prepared, he gave her the good news. News that stopped her in her tracks.

"I who speak to you am he" (v. 26).

Jesus chose to reveal his true identity at the strangest times to the most unexpected people. The religious leaders in Jerusalem tried every trick in their book to get a straight answer from him on this subject. He always responded by telling a story, asking a question, or just changing the subject. But now, in the middle of nowhere, Jesus revealed his identity to a Samaritan woman who wasn't even asking. But deep down in that mysterious place of knowing, she knew that Jesus had just told the truth. Her parched soul got its very first taste of water. Her hope was not in vain after all. She had found living water.

~~~

Their conversation was interrupted by voices coming from the direction of Sychar. The disciples returned from the town with a small feast in their arms. The sight of Jesus talking with a woman—especially a Samaritan woman—surprised them, but no one said a word. As they began preparations for their noon meal, the woman rose and began her long walk back into town. But as John is quick to point out, she left her water jar by the side of the well.

What she did next required a great deal of courage on her part. Upon entering the city, she went immediately to the elders. "Come, see a man who told me everything I ever did. Could this be the Christ?" (John 4:29). The men probably burst out laughing. "Everyone knows everything you ever did! It doesn't take a prophet to figure that out!" But their laughter was short-lived. She wasn't cowering. Apparently, she wasn't kidding. And something was different. No one could dismiss the transparency of her excitement, so they followed the woman to the outskirts of town.

According to John, an eyewitness to the event, Jesus and his disciples stayed in Sychar two more days. The result was that "many of the Samaritans from that town believed in him because of the woman's testimony, 'He told me everything I ever did'" (John 4:39).

~~~

I include this seemingly random encounter with Jesus because it introduces us to an important expression of God's grace. And perhaps that is why John included it as well. The setup to the story says it best: "He had to pass through Samaria." As we saw earlier, he didn't really have to. Most Jews didn't. Jesus chose to go to an out-of-the-way town to extend grace to an out-of-the-way woman. Grace in the form of new life. New life that did not erase her old life. New life that did not justify her old life. This was new life that would sustain her in spite of her past life and throughout the rest of her life. Certainly Jesus' offer of eternal life included forgiveness. But this was bigger than that. This was an offer of *in-spite-of* grace. She found peace and joy *in spite of* all she had been through. Peace that was disconnected from her unpeaceful surroundings. But peace that connected deeply with her soul.

At last she was able to face those who knew everything she ever did. But not by hiding behind a mask of indifference. She could face those who knew her best because she was now able to face herself. Gone was the need to excuse. Gone was the self-deception. Shame, her constant companion, was nowhere to be found. Nothing had changed. But she had changed. She had new life. Eternal life. Life that intersected with this life in an unexplainable way. Eternal life that didn't erase the reality of this life but removed the sting. It was exactly what she needed. But it was something she wasn't sure existed. This was God's carrying grace. His sustaining grace.

~~~

Life has a way of leaving us thirsty. The years leave us with unfulfilled longings. Aches. Unfulfilled dreams. Missed opportunities. Regardless of what kind of life we've led, eventually we bump up against something that just won't move. Something we cannot change. Consequences of our own making. Consequences of someone else's making. All of us would like to go back to a day, a weekend, or a season of our lives and do things differently. In some cases we would like to go back in time and urge someone we love to do things differently. But time only moves in one direction. So while we are tempted to look back, we can never go back. And it's the looking back that surfaces our thirst, a thirst that seems unquenchable.

As the woman from Sychar discovered, **God's response to the thirsty soul is grace**. We would prefer time travel. Second chances. Do overs. But God opts for sustaining grace. Grace that leverages the past for a better future. Grace that fills the gaps created by our sin or the sin of others. Grace that allows us to honestly face and carry our pasts but without being controlled by them. Grace that makes denial unnecessary.

The writer of Hebrews refers to it this way: "Let us then approach the throne of grace with confidence, so that we may receive mercy and find grace to help us in our time of need" (4:16). I don't think it is intuitive to pray for grace and mercy in our time of need. We pray for the thing we *need* in our time of need. We pray for circumstances to change. We pray for memories to go away. We pray for people to treat us better. And so we should. But none of that is promised. What's promised is grace and mercy in our time of need.

The apostle Paul introduced his Corinthian audience to God's sustaining grace by telling them a story about his personal struggle with what seems to have been a physical malady of some kind. According to his story, he prayed for God to remove whatever it was. God said no. That's actually encouraging. If God said no to Paul, that makes it a little easier for me to take no for an answer too.

Instead of changing whatever it was that Paul wanted changed, God gave him sustaining grace: "But he said to me, 'My grace is sufficient for you, for my power is made perfect in weakness'" (2 Cor. 12:9). The implications are clear. "Paul, your weakness isn't going away. But I'm going to sustain you through it. How? Grace." The phrase "my power" connects us right back to the experience of the woman from Sychar. "My power" implies the presence of God. The constant presence of God. This is reiterated by the verb *is* in the phrase "my grace is sufficient." As in every day, all the time. As Jesus offered the woman of Sychar a well of living water that would constantly be springing up to provide her with new life, so God promised Paul a constant stream of divine strength to enable him to manage through a weakness that was not going away.

The grace of God is not limited to an act of God at the time of our salvation. **The grace of God is the life of the Savior coursing through the souls of believers to sustain us through those things that will not or cannot change.** It is a well of living water. It is God's power manifest in our weakness. In this way the grace of God is a constant reminder of the presence of God. If you have ever gone through a difficult season of life and felt as if God carried you through it, then you have experienced this form of grace. Perhaps you've watched in amazement as a Christian friend walked through a dark valley relationally, physically, or financially and yet maintained his or her peace. That's God's *in-spite-of* grace. The grace to endure. It's tempting to think that someone who is able to maintain peace in the midst of a personal storm is simply in denial. But as a pastor I've seen God's sustaining grace at work in the lives of so many people on so many occasions that I know it's real. The apostle Paul said it best. He referred to it as a peace that surpasses or "transcends" all human understanding (Phil. 4:7). That peace, he said, actually guards our hearts and minds. He was so confident in this expression of God's grace that he told the Philippian believers "to be anxious for nothing." That's a pretty insensitive thing to say, unless you are absolutely confident that God's grace will be sufficient for whatever someone is facing. He was. And we can be as well.

Perhaps, like the woman from Sychar, you are wondering, *How do I get this living water? How do I get some of this* in-spite-of *grace?* While there is no formula, John leaves us with several clues in the narrative.

The appropriation of God's grace begins with acknowledgment of Jesus as God's Son. When Jesus announced to the woman at Sychar that he was indeed the long-awaited Messiah, she had a decision to make: to believe or not to believe. She believed, and that put the wheels of grace in motion. And so it is with each of us. Grace begins with faith—a decision to believe that Jesus is who he says he is. For those of us living on this side of Jesus' death and resurrection, grace begins with the decision to put our trust in his death on the cross for the payment of our sin. But it doesn't end there.

Like the woman from Sychar, we have all developed ways of coping with our past and ways of coping with our current circumstances. We all have approaches for coping with the uncertainties of tomorrow. Sustaining grace becomes a reality only after we have put away our inappropriate, self-serving, coping mechanisms. I think this is why Jesus dug around in the woman's past. To resurface what had been there all along: thirst. Thirst for forgiveness. But beyond that, he resurfaced thirst for the ability to face her past and cope with the present. For Jesus to quench her thirst, she needed to feel it. So in his own way he exposed and then pushed aside her coping mechanisms. He wanted to bring grace to the point of her greatest thirst. But to do that, she needed to be thirsty.

The same is true for us. We can't receive God's forgiving grace while continuing to prop ourselves up through denial and self-effort. To experience God's *in-spite-of* grace we must allow ourselves to feel the thirst created by our past. The past must be embraced before it can be overcome. Then we must declare our weaknesses and our need for God's sustaining strength in our present circumstances. As Paul said, it is only when we are weak that he can be strong through us. Culture teaches us to hide our weaknesses. Culture encourages us to compensate for our weaknesses. Jesus encourages us to acknowledge our weaknesses and then cling to him for the grace to function in spite of them. When you acknowledge you are weak, that is an invitation to your Savior to be strong through you. **A declaration of thirst is an invitation for God to quench your thirst.**

For years I've prayed and taught people to pray, *Heavenly Father, I cannot, but you can. I cannot, but you can. In my weakness, be strong.* This is different from promising God how much better you intend to be and how much harder you intend to try. Again, it is only when and where you are weak that he has the opportunity to be strong. Only then can his grace be sufficient for you. Only then will his power be made perfect in your weakness.

As we close this chapter, I want to encourage you to do something that may feel a bit strange. Assuming you are alone, say the following out loud: "Heavenly Father, I cannot, but you can." One more time, "Heavenly Father, I cannot, but you can." I have found that there is something powerful about expressing this out loud. Now take it a step further. Add some specifics. What is it you find just about impossible to do? What is that set of circumstances you find it almost impossible to cope with? What is it that's driving you to drink or medicate too much? Out loud, fill in the blank and declare, "Heavenly Father, I cannot _____, but I believe you can."

Beginning your day with a declaration of your weakness and your reliance upon the grace of God is perhaps one of the best habits you will ever take up. It is a declaration that you need rivers of living water to bubble up and flow through your heart, mind, and emotions. It is an acknowledgment that you believe God is able and willing to sustain you *in spite of* what's happened in the past and what's happening around you now. As this becomes part of your daily routine, you will learn to relax in and rely on God's sustaining grace.

CHAPTER 12

Saved by Grace

Grace is not ours to earn; it is God's to give.

By five in the morning, several dozen men had come to the empty lot next to the town's only convenience store. In clusters of three, four, and five, they sipped coffee and talked, occasionally glancing toward the main road for an opportunity to work. Bob's mud-spattered pickup attracted their attention right away as he pulled alongside the curb.

Bob had recently purchased a large parcel of neglected, overgrown farmland just south of town. He planned to establish a huge greenhouse and nursery to serve the suburban sprawl steadily creeping north from the big city, but the fence lines and outbuildings were covered in a tangle of kudzu and wisteria. He offered to pay five men $100 each for twelve hours of cutting and clearing, and before he could finish a sentence, five eager laborers piled into the bed of his truck. Within half an hour, the workers—equipped with gloves and cutting tools—were busy hacking away at the thick layer of vegetation. Bob designated the oldest man foreman and left him in charge before running a few errands.

Three hours later, Bob returned to the property with water. He noticed an impressive mound of greenery beside the road but could barely tell where the men had been working. Clearly, the job would require more hands than he had anticipated. He left the coolers of ice water under a shade tree and headed straight for the empty lot in town. He doubled the crew, leaving ten men on the job before heading off to a meeting with the town manager.

Upon returning to the property at noon, he added five more workers, and then again at three. Still, with twenty men chopping and pulling vines, Bob worried that the project would fall behind schedule. So, at five in the evening, he put five more men to work.

By six o'clock, Bob decided to accept the truth he had been avoiding. Clearing the land would require heavy equipment. After a quick trip to the bank, he returned to the property with a handful of cash. He instructed the foreman, "Pay the men for the day, starting with the last crew first."

With a sharp whistle and a wave from the foreman, the men lined up for their wages. The workers who arrived at five in the evening were delighted to receive a crisp $100 bill after just one hour of labor. Word of Bob's generosity quickly passed to the back of the line, where the original five began to calculate and celebrate. Their smiles faded, however, when the foreman handed each a crisp $100 bill.

"Wait a minute," said one laborer on behalf of all. "You gotta be kidding!"

Bob overheard the outburst. "Is there a problem?" he asked.

"We worked ourselves nearly to death for twelve hours! The guys at the front of the line got the same amount for an hour of work."

Bob stuck his hands in his jeans, looked at the ground for a moment, and then peered at the man from beneath his eyebrows. "Tell me, friend. Did we not agree on $100 for a twelve-hour day?"

"Yeah, but . . ."

"And you have the money you were promised, right?"

"Well, yeah. Technically, that's right, but . . ."

Bob put up his hand to silence the spokesman. "Then we're all square. Is there a rule that says I can't pay people what I want to with my own money?"

If you're tempted to side with the workers in this story, you're not alone. This slightly modified parable of Jesus—originally recorded by Matthew (20:1–16)—has challenged readers for more than two thousand years. The landowner's pay scale violates our sense of fair play. We are bothered by what Philip Yancey describes as "the scandalous mathematics of grace."[1] But even then, we can hardly argue with the foreman's logic.

As every parent knows, fairness is a tricky thing. There are always two sides to fairness. If I had been part of the team that worked all day, I would have felt it was unfair to be paid the same as the latecomers. But if I were Bob, I would have felt it was unfair if I wasn't allowed to be generous with my money. As Philip Yancey put it, their discontentment rose from the scandalous mathematics of grace.

Now here's the really interesting thing. Jesus said this parable reflects what the kingdom of heaven is like (Matt. 20:1). It's unfair. The kingdom of heaven is unfair. At least the way most of us measure fairness. So next time one of your kids complains, "That's not fair," just tell 'em, "Neither is the kingdom of heaven." I should probably write a parenting book next.

Again, fairness is a tricky thing. Here's something I've noticed: I only complain about things being unfair when unfair works against me. When unfairness works to my advantage, I call that answered prayer. How do you respond when you get more than your fair share of something good? Do you turn it down? Of course not. You are like me. You thank God and keep moving before somebody changes his mind. You've never said, "No fair! My piece is bigger than everyone else's." I've never heard one of my children say, "No fair! I got to sit in the front seat last time. Somebody else should get a turn!" When it comes to fairness, we are all a bit selective.

Fortunately for us, the kingdom of God does not operate according to the principles of fairness. At least not the way we measure fairness. When I think about all the things I've done wrong, when I consider all the times I've promised God I wouldn't and then did, I've concluded that I don't really *want* God to be fair in the fairest sense of the term. If fair means I get what I deserve, I don't really want fair. I would opt for grace instead. I bet you feel the same way.

The kingdom of God is not fair in the sense that everybody gets what he or she deserves. It's not fair the way the guys who worked twelve hours measured fairness. The kingdom of God is fair the way Bob measured fairness. God gets to give what he wants to whom he wants to give. God laid aside fairness in its purest form (i.e., everybody gets what they deserve), and opted for fairness in the sense of it being fair for him to extend mercy and grace if he wants to. But as we will see, that's oversimplifying a bit.

⁓〇

Now a parable about kingdom fairness is one thing. But seeing this unusual value system fleshed out in real life is another thing altogether. So hang on.

If you are familiar with the New Testament, you have probably heard the story of Stephen, the first Christian martyr. The church was still new when Stephen put his trust in Christ. The Christian community in Jerusalem enjoyed a wonderful time of unity despite their remarkable diversity. Nearly all the early Christians were Jewish believers, attending temple services on the Sabbath and meeting in homes for prayer and meals during the week. Some were Jewish by birth, others by conversion. But they embraced one another as family, referring to each other as brother and sister in greetings.

But all good things must come to an end. Luke writes, "In those days when the number of disciples was increasing, the Grecian Jews among them complained against the Hebraic Jews because their widows were being overlooked in the daily distribution of food" (Acts 6:1). How interesting. The first fight recorded in church history was a food fight. The Jewish converts from outside of Palestine weren't getting the same attention as those who were from the area.

To address the problem, Jesus' disciples instructed the congregation to select seven qualified men to oversee the food distribution. Stephen's name emerged first. Known for his faith, this Gentile convert to Judaism who later embraced Jesus as the Messiah enjoyed the confidence of everyone in the church.

He proved to be a faithful minister within the community as well as a strong voice of reason against outside opposition. Synagogue leaders challenged the church, but Stephen's knowledge of the Scriptures and his skill in debate proved too effective. "They could not stand up against his wisdom or the Spirit by whom he spoke" (Acts 6:10). Unable to defeat him openly with reason, the enemies of the church resorted to treachery.

Stephen's enemies accused him of blasphemy against Moses, and they formally charged him before the Jewish court, the Sanhedrin. To support their case, they found false witnesses willing to perjure themselves, testifying, "This fellow never stops speaking against this holy place and against the law. For we have heard him say that this Jesus of Nazareth will destroy this place and change the customs Moses handed down to us" (Acts 6:13–14).

The courage of most men would have withered before the hostile power of the Sanhedrin. This, remember, was the same governmental body that condemned Jesus and convinced Rome to crucify him. Yet Stephen stood his ground rather than trying to save himself. At the end of a stirring speech in which he demonstrated conclusively that rejecting Jesus and clinging to the Law makes a person an idolater, Stephen bravely told the truth, saying, "You stiff-necked people, with uncircumcised hearts and ears! You are just like your fathers: You always resist the Holy Spirit! Was there ever a prophet your fathers did not persecute? They even killed those who predicted the coming of the Righteous One. And now you have betrayed and murdered him— you who have received the law that was put into effect through angels but have not obeyed it" (Acts 7:51–53).

The dignified gathering of Israel's most influential men suddenly turned into a raving mob. They seized Stephen, dragged him outside the walls of the city, and began crushing him with stones. With his life ebbing away, the young man cried out, "Lord, do not hold this sin against them" (Acts 7:60).

As the early church's first martyr, he became a hero of the faith. If anyone deserved to go to heaven, it would be Stephen. He led an exemplary life and died a champion of faith.

Later known as the apostle Paul, Saul was a stark contrast to Stephen. Describing himself before becoming a Christian, he wrote, "If anyone else thinks he has reasons to put confidence in [human standards of goodness], I have more: circumcised on the eighth day, of the people of Israel, of the tribe of Benjamin, a Hebrew of Hebrews; in regard to the law, a Pharisee; as for zeal, persecuting the church; as for legalistic righteousness, faultless" (Phil. 3:4–6). By every standard of Jewish goodness, Saul ranked among the best. He was born into the race God had chosen to receive his blessing and through which he planned to bless the world. Saul obeyed the law of God more consistently than any of his law-abiding peers. And no one could match Saul's sincerity or zeal. Yet his love for the law of God and the passion of his convictions led him to murder.

He openly admitted, "I persecuted the church of God and tried to destroy it. I was advancing in Judaism beyond many Jews of my own age and was extremely zealous for the traditions of my fathers" (Gal. 1:13–14). Saul was present the day the mob stoned Stephen to death. He watched with approval as a truly righteous man gave away his life for what he believed. Many years later, Saul, then Paul, admitted to a close friend, "I was once a blasphemer and a persecutor and a violent man" (1 Tim. 1.13).

While hunting down Christians in order to throw them in prison, Paul experienced a defining moment. A direct encounter with the Son of God caused him to realize that his good deeds were, in fact, grievous sins. That very day, Paul gave up trusting in his own personal righteousness and received God's grace and forgiveness, as well as a new name. He recognized Christ as his Messiah and Savior and joined the ranks of the Christians he had been persecuting.

Paul became a tireless Christian missionary. He traveled throughout the eastern Roman Empire for fifteen years, logging more than twenty thousand miles, preaching, teaching, establishing churches, and writing nearly one-third of what became the New Testament. He endured hardship to advance the gospel. He suffered unjust persecution, false accusation, stoning, scourging, and imprisonment in service to Jesus Christ. Before his martyrdom in Rome, Paul did more to expand the kingdom of God than any other person in the first century.

Unlike Stephen's relatively wholesome youth, violence and hatred stained the early part of Paul's life. Fortunately, he lived long enough and worked hard enough to erase his past sins in the minds of most. He was accepted into the Christian community and, like Stephen, became a hero of the faith. He lived the second half of his life with absolute confidence that death would usher him into the presence of God, in spite of his past life (2 Cor. 5:8).

But before either Stephen or Paul burst onto the scene, there was another man whose faith in Christ made him somewhat famous. He is certainly no hero of the faith, yet his story is told and retold wherever the gospel is preached. We don't know his name. But we know his character—and apparently he was quite a character. We know very little about his past, other than he is described as a criminal. When we are introduced, his story is in the final pages of its final chapter: he was hanging on a cross within earshot of Jesus.

The fact that he was described as a criminal rather than a zealot or a slave indicates that he was guilty of crimes so heinous that he couldn't even be trusted to row a Roman warship. Romans rarely forfeited a potential rower unless he was too violent or too unpredictable to control. Such was the nature of this man. Luke describes the scene as follows:

> Two other men, both criminals, were also led out with him to be executed. When they came to the place called the Skull, there they crucified him, along with the criminals—one on his right, the other on his left. (Luke 23:32–33)

Curiosity seekers looked on from a distance. Religious authorities stopped by to sneer, "He saved others; let him save himself if he is the Christ of God, the Chosen One" (Luke 23:35). The soldiers mocked, "If you are the king of the Jews, save yourself" (v. 37). Eventually, one of the men crucified beside Jesus joined in as well, "Aren't you the Christ? Save yourself and us!" (v. 39).

Then, quite unexpectedly, someone came to Jesus' defense. A most unlikely someone. The other criminal. Strange when you think about it. This was the only person to come to Jesus' defense. He interrupted the stream of cursing and epithets with a question and a confession: "Don't you fear God . . . since you are under the same sentence? We are punished justly, for we are getting what our deeds deserve. But this man has done nothing wrong" (Luke 23:40–41).

Clearly the criminal believed in God. He recognized his own guilt. By his own admission he deserved death. By his own admission he deserved to be crucified. He had no illusions about deserving anything good in the life to come. If there was an afterlife, he knew it was nothing he should be looking forward to. His only hope, if there was any hope, was what he deserved least and had extended very little of in his miserable life: mercy and grace. So in an act of desperation, he cried out, "Jesus, remember me when you come into your kingdom" (Luke 23:42).

If the kingdom of heaven was reserved for good people, this man didn't have a prayer. Well, he had a prayer, but he didn't have a chance. Repentance from a cross is meaningless. Rededication when you only have hours to live doesn't count for anything. We are all sorry once we are facing the penalty of our actions. There was nothing to promise. He had nothing to offer. Restitution for his crimes was impossible. He had no bargaining power. He had earned the cross, and he had earned an eternity separated from all that was good. He was on his way to receiving exactly what he deserved.

But then Jesus disturbed the proper order of things. He interfered with this man's karma. **He trumped justice as justice was understood. He decided to be extravagantly unfair.**

"Jesus answered him" (Luke 23:43).

Are you kidding? Jesus answered him? I love those three words. Why bother? Why acknowledge him? Why recognize the existence of such a person? Every word Jesus spoke from the cross cost him physically. Every breath caused unimaginable pain as he pushed and pulled on nail-pierced extremities to exhale. But Jesus answered him anyway: "I tell you the truth, today you will be with me in paradise" (Luke 23:43).

Now, I know you've probably heard this story before, but let's not rush by this too quickly. Jesus, God in a body, perfection in skin, holiness with hands and feet, promised a man who was as opposite him as opposite could be, "Where I'm going, you're going." How could that be? Jesus granted the eleventh-hour convert the same eternal reward as Stephen! That's not fair. Stephen was executed because of his righteousness. This man was being executed for his crimes. A few years later they would be joined by the apostle Paul—Paul, who was imprisoned, stoned, shipwrecked, snakebit, beat, and finally beheaded because of his relentless desire to export the message of Jesus all over the known world. So why would a criminal be granted entrance into the kingdom of God along with men like Stephen and Paul? That's really not fair.

In fact it's better than fair.

It's grace.

~◌

I know this is naive, but I really don't understand why people are so resistant to the gospel. I realize it has been mischaracterized through the years. Some of us Christians certainly haven't helped the cause with our less-than-consistent behavior. But once someone gets past *us* and looks at the offer of grace, it just seems too good to pass up. When one stops to consider the implications of the exchange between the criminal and Jesus, it is quite astonishing. Why would anyone opt for a religious system based on personal performance? Who thinks they are really good enough to earn heaven? And then there's the question, *earn it based on what?* There really isn't an objective standard of behavior to go by. Americans like to lean into the Ten Commandments as the standard. But as we've discussed, the Ten Commandments weren't given for that purpose. So where does one even go to find out how good you have to be?

Christians, Jews, Muslims, Hindus . . . all have versions of the golden rule. But that's a pretty high standard to attain consistently. Which brings up an issue no one likes to talk about: Is 70 percent a passing grade for heaven? If I do unto others as I want them to do unto me 70 percent of the time, am I in? Sixty percent? What about family? Does the same percentage apply toward relatives, or does it drop a few percentage points?

As silly as it starts to get, I think those are relevant questions for anyone who thinks he can behave his way into God's good graces. If God is looking for good people, then we need to know what's good and where the pass/fail line is. In *The Abolition of Man*, C. S. Lewis lists eight teachings found among the religious literature of the American Indians, the ancient Greeks, the ancient Chinese, Judaism, and Christianity. I guess in addition to the golden rule, these would be good things to pay attention to:

- Don't harm others with word or deed.
- Honor your parents.
- Be kind to siblings and the elderly.
- Be honest in all your dealings.
- Don't lie.
- Don't have sex with another person's spouse.
- Care for those who are weaker.
- Put others first.[2]

The other thing those religions share is the assumption that people will fail to adhere to those eight commands. Everybody in every religion eventually falls short on some point. We know that to be the case, because all these systems offer advice on what to do when a person messes up. But that's where the common ground ends. At that point, each has its own approach to making up for failure to adhere to the rules. So to summarize:

- There is a God.
- God has a standard for individuals to live by.
- But it's too hard.
- Good luck!
- See you on the other side . . . maybe.

Religion highlights our inability to live up to a divine standard, thus creating a gap. But experience does as well. **We fall short of our own expectations; we don't need religion to tell us that we really aren't all that good.** We've all had to say, "I'm sorry" or "I was wrong." Once we fail, there's something in us that prompts us to try to make up for our failures with better behavior, generosity, or promises. And while we can do better going forward, there's nothing we can do about the past. We can't go back and be a better parent, better husband, or better wife. We can't go back and un-cheat, un-lie, un-addict. Being perfect going forward doesn't erase the past.

That's what makes Christianity so unique. That's what makes grace so powerful. Jesus came into the world and did what nobody else could do. He affirmed the list. He kept the Law. He declared God's law good. But then he offered himself as the answer to the question no one else could answer: "Now that I've messed up, what do I do?" What the rules and the rule givers could not do, Jesus did by laying down his life as the full and final sacrifice for sin. **Christ's death and resurrection signaled to the world that the kingdom of God is not reserved for good people. It is reserved for forgiven people.**

Good forgiven people. Pretty good forgiven people. Not-so-good forgiven people. And people like the criminal on the cross who didn't have any good to bargain with.

And that brings us back around to *fair*.

⁘

The gospel is actually the fairest system imaginable. It's fairer than fair. Think about it:

- Everybody is invited.
- Everybody gets in the same way.
- Everybody can meet the requirement.

Everybody is invited. Judah was invited along with Rahab, David, and Nicodemus. Everybody gets in the same way—through Christ. His death paid for the sins of the world, including the sins of all those Old Testament characters whom God chose solely because of his grace. Everybody can meet the requirement, faith. By faith Abraham was declared righteous. By faith the woman of Sychar received eternal life.

But this kind of fair didn't come without a price. Jesus bled and died to open the kingdom's doors wide enough for all of us good and not-so-good people to enter. Grace was costly. But it was not costly to us. It was the sacrificial death of Jesus that gave God the latitude to grant the Stephens, Sauls, and last-minute converts of the world the same eternal home. And it was Christ's death on the cross that makes the kingdom of God available to you and me as well. Is that fair?

No. It's far better than fair.

It's grace.

CHAPTER 13

Commissioned for Grace

Grace plus anything is anything but grace.

I grew up going to church. My father is a pastor. He's pastored the same church in Atlanta for more than forty years. After college I went to graduate school to study theology. Upon graduating I landed a job back at my dad's church. They needed someone to work with high school students. I still acted like one, so it was perfect. I served under his leadership for ten years before joining a group of friends to launch North Point Community Church. I've been a pastor for more than twenty-five years now. I love the local church. Looking back over my years as an attendee, preacher's kid, staff member, and church planter, I'm absolutely convinced that **the church is most appealing when the message of grace is most apparent**. Similarly, the church is most effective when the message of grace is most evident.

When I meet someone who doesn't attend church, I almost always ask why. I rarely get a theological answer. No one has ever responded with, "Because I don't believe the Bible is true," though that's true for a lot of people. Heck, I know people who *go* to church who don't believe the entire Bible is true.

What I normally hear are things like, "Well, I just don't have time," or "We just haven't found a church that's right for us," or "I really should, but . . ." My favorite answer came from a doctor. I asked, "Do you attend church anywhere?" He replied, "Not anymore, I already did that." Curious, I asked what he meant. He said, "For twenty-eight years, I got up every Sunday and went to church. I taught boys' Sunday school. I was a deacon. Then, one Sunday morning, I got up and thought to myself, *I'm done*. I told my wife, 'We're done with that,' and I went to play golf. And I've been playing golf every Sunday morning since."

Wasn't much I could say to that. He had put in his time, punched out, and never looked back. It's kind of strange when you think about it. Most Americans who don't attend church don't attend for reasons that have nothing to do with God *per se*. In fact, the people I talk to don't have a problem with God. They just don't go to church.

Churches fill up on Christmas and Easter. It's as if people show up to see if anything has changed. When they discover it hasn't, they don't come back. Respect for God keeps 'em in the holiday cycle. But that's about it. There are exceptions, of course. Personal and even national tragedy has a way of driving people back to church. In 1944, when President Roosevelt announced that our soldiers were storming the beaches of France, thousands of Americans stopped what they were doing and went to church in the middle of the week. Special services were held in just about every church. Pews were jammed with worshippers.

Similarly, on the morning of September 11, 2001, after the magnitude and significance of what was taking place became clear, I gathered my staff and said, "We need to be prepared. This coming Sunday will be bigger than Easter." And it was. Churches all over America were overflowing. People needed assurance, so they flocked to church. But two weeks later, attendance patterns were back to normal. I suppose people got what they came for. Others were reminded of why they had quit going in the first place. Clearly, there was no compelling reason to keep coming back.

Church and parish leaders are quick to blame a lack of church attendance on a lack of commitment among their flocks and society in general. But blaming followers for not following is a declaration of failed leadership. **If people aren't following, it's because someone's not leading.** Besides, people don't have a problem with commitment. They are committed to all kinds of things. They just aren't committed to church. As one guy told me, "Church is for church people. I'm not really a church person."

As strange as that may sound to "church people," I think that's a pretty common attitude. And it makes a lot of sense. Church is for church people like golf is for golfers, hunting is for hunters, coin collecting is for coin collectors, and bridge is for . . . people who play bridge. You get the point. From the public's perspective, church is just another thing to do on a day when there are plenty of other things to do.

∼⌒

For some, that line of reasoning doesn't stop there. If church is for church people, then the message of Jesus must be for church people as well. And if the message of Jesus is exclusively for church people, then so is the message of grace. But, of course, nothing could be further from the truth. As we've seen, Jesus went out of his way to introduce his Father's grace to those who were far from God and excluded from religious life. As if his example were not enough, on the day of his departure he *commanded* his little band of followers to take his message of grace to every nation (Matt. 28:19). As prepared as his closest followers should have been for an assignment like that, it still came as a big surprise. Here's why.

Throughout Jesus' earthly ministry, he spoke frequently of the kingdom of God and the kingdom of heaven. Consequently, his followers expected him to establish a kingdom. But Jesus had something else in mind. Instead of establishing a kingdom, he planted the church. The Greek term translated *church* simply means "a gathering." In this case, it would be a gathering with a very specific purpose. They were to take his message to all nations. Here's Luke's version of a portion of Jesus' final instructions: "But you will receive power when the Holy Spirit comes on you; and you will be my witnesses in Jerusalem, and in all Judea and Samaria, and to the ends of the earth" (Acts 1:8). This new gathering—later referred to as the church—was established by Jesus as the vehicle for delivering the message of grace to "the ends of the earth."

Now, think about that for a moment. Jesus asked his followers to be intentional about taking his message to nonreligious people as well as to people who had embraced different religious systems. He believed his message was transcultural and transgenerational. He saw no problem asking people of different faiths and worldviews to consider his message of forgiveness and grace. And no wonder; as we discovered in the previous chapter, he had come with the solution to the problem every religion recognized and wrestled with: sin. Failure to keep the rules. His was a message for all people of all nations regardless of religious or nonreligious affiliation. It was this unique message that would be the fulfillment of God's promise to Abraham hundreds of years earlier when he said that through him all the nations of the earth would be blessed.

~⟶⟶⟶)

If the church is God's primary vehicle for dispensing the message of grace, then the local church is clearly not for church people. It's for everybody. If the prevailing view of culture is that church is for church people, then the church has failed in its mission. The need for grace certainly hasn't diminished. Everybody still needs forgiveness. Everybody wonders at some time where he stands with God and if that's something he can even know. The local church may have lost its appeal, but grace certainly hasn't.

If people think church is for church people, then we church people need to reexamine our messaging. When grace is no longer front and center in the messaging and programming of a church, something else is. Something less than grace. And as history has borne witness to time and time again, the church can become a graceless place.

People were drawn to Jesus. As we discovered with Matthew, people who were nothing like Jesus liked Jesus. As his body, as his hands and feet, as his representatives on the planet, the same should be true of us. And while that is true of some churches, it is not true of the majority. But this is not a new problem. Graceless church raised its ugly head about fifteen minutes after Jesus said his final farewell.

Okay. Maybe not fifteen minutes. But sooner than you might expect.

~⟶⟶⟶)

The New Testament book of Acts tells the story of the formation and development of the early church. Things got off to an incredible start. Within the first few days, thousands of men and women in Jerusalem put their faith in Christ as Savior and Messiah. The entire region was alive with stories of miracles and personal transformation. Before long evangelists were leaving Jerusalem to take the message of Jesus' death and resurrection to surrounding villages and towns.

And then something quite unexpected happened. Gentiles started to believe as well. Once they believed, they wanted to join the celebration—primarily Jewish celebration. But the majority of Jewish Christians were not quite ready for that. Jesus was *their* Messiah. After all, he was Jewish. Most of his teaching revolved around the kingdom of God, and every good Jew knew that was synonymous with the kingdom of Israel.

Then things really got out of hand. Some of the original apostles became intentional with their Gentile evangelistic efforts. They traveled to predominantly Gentile areas and proclaimed the resurrection of Jesus. Just about everywhere they went, people believed. As these new believers began to find one another, local gatherings, or churches, were formed. Leaders were chosen. But this didn't sit well with traditionally minded believing Jews. And that's understandable.

To the outside world, Christianity was viewed as a sect within Judaism. First-century believing Jews didn't consider themselves converts to something new. Jesus was their Jewish Messiah. If anybody was a convert, it was the Gentiles. They were the ones crashing the party.

In truth, Christianity is an extension of Judaism. As we've discovered, much of the Old Testament points to the coming of a Messiah. David was promised an heir who would reign forever. Isaiah told of a suffering deliverer who would carry the sins of the world. Even Jesus' cousin John referred to him as the Lamb of God—a clear connection to the Jewish sacrificial system. So it is easy to understand why first-century Jewish-Christians felt a little threatened by this sudden influx of nonpracticing outsiders.

To complicate matters even more, the Gentile believers brought their Gentile customs, habits, and values right along with them. Problem was, many of their Gentile ways were highly offensive to the

Jews. Beyond offensive, some of their practices were outright sacrilegious. Especially their eating habits. To make matters worse, most of the early Christians, being Jewish, met at local synagogues. Suddenly there were handfuls of Gentiles showing up and wanting to participate. But they knew nothing about how to keep the Sabbath. They knew nothing about ceremonial cleansing. It was a mess.

The only plausible solution was to require Gentile Christians to become Jewish. These new converts to Christianity would need to convert to Judaism as a first step toward becoming a follower of Christ, or "the Way," as it was commonly referred to (Acts 19:23). Now, if becoming Jewish meant simply being schooled in the Jewish Scriptures and Hebrew theology, that probably would not have been a big deal. Unfortunately for the men, it meant more than that. A lot more. Becoming Jewish would require surgery! If you think membership standards in your church are high, think again. The most ardent supporters of the Jewish-First movement taught the following: "Unless you are circumcised, according to the custom taught by Moses, you cannot be saved" (Acts 15:1). Bottom line, the new-members classes were full of women and children while the men waited in the car.

But circumcision was only the beginning.

In addition to circumcision, Gentile believers would be required to submit to the entire Law of Moses. Keeping the Law was hard for the average Jew, in spite of having been raised with it. For an adult Gentile whose lifestyle had been shaped predominantly by Greek and Roman values and traditions, this was going to be an impossible task. Just learning the Law could take years. If all of that was a precursor to following Jesus, who could do it?

As this new standard for membership was beginning to be

propagated in a few areas, the church continued to flourish just about everywhere the message of Jesus was being preached. This was especially true in the Gentile city of Antioch, located about three hundred miles north of Jerusalem. The apostle Paul had settled there with another teacher named Barnabas. Together they taught, and many non-Jewish people responded to the offer of salvation. In fact, it was in Antioch that the term *Christian* was first used to describe followers of Jesus (Acts 11:26).

Eventually, reports filtered into Jerusalem that scores of Gentiles in Antioch were becoming Christians with no consideration for becoming Jewish. This was disturbing to the traditionalists among the Jewish Christians, so they appointed a committee and sent them to Antioch to set things straight. Which, of course, only made things worse.

As disturbing as the circumcision component of their message was, there was actually something even more insidious at work. By insisting that non-Jews become Jews, they were diluting the essence of Jesus' message. Salvation was no longer a gift; it was something a person worked for and earned. Once again, no one would really know where he stood with God. Christianity was on the path to becoming just another graceless religion.

To resolve the conflict, the church leaders in Antioch appointed Barnabas, Paul, and a few others as envoys to Jerusalem, where they would get official clarification from the apostles. In those days there was no pope or bishop to appeal to. There was no formal hierarchal structure at all. Local churches operated as autonomous local congregations. However, as churches sprang up across the Roman Empire, they looked to the apostles for leadership. After all, these men had spent three years listening to and watching Jesus. If anyone would know what to do with this influx of Gentiles, they would.

When the group from Antioch arrived in Jerusalem, they received a warm reception. Barnabas and Paul reported on the extraordinary growth of the church. They specifically highlighted the large number of Gentiles who were embracing the message of Christ. When they finished their report, their opponents stood and declared, "The Gentiles must be circumcised and required to obey the law of Moses" (Acts 15:5). Luke tells us that many of those who stood against Paul and Barnabas were actually Pharisees who had become believers. But as ardent followers of the Law, they just couldn't give it up. Apparently these Christian Pharisees had come to faith after the resurrection. Consequently, they were not as familiar with the teachings of Jesus as the others.

After a lengthy debate, Peter addressed the group. He began by reminding them of his own experience with Gentiles and the gospel. God had made it abundantly clear to Peter that salvation was to be offered to everyone on the same terms: faith in Christ. Peter reasoned, "He made no distinction between us and them [Gentiles], for he purified their hearts by faith. Now then, why do you try to test God by putting on the necks of the disciples a yoke that neither we nor our fathers have been able to bear?" (Acts 15:9–10). Translated: "My Jewish friends, who are we kidding? We don't even keep the Law all that well. It's a yoke we would gladly rid ourselves of. So why burden the Gentiles with it?" That was a pretty compelling argument. Peter continued, "No! We believe it is through the *grace* of our Lord Jesus that we are saved, just as they are" (v. 11; emphasis added). This was a straight-up battle for grace. **Peter knew that if you start shaving layers off of grace, it's no longer grace. And if you start adding things to grace, it's no longer grace either.**

When Peter was finished, all eyes turned to James. James, the brother of Jesus, was the most influential church leader in Jerusalem. He rose to address the group. His words carried immense weight. Like the Pharisees, James came to faith late. Apparently he, too, was convinced of Jesus' true identity only after the resurrection. Like Peter, he believed non-Jewish believers should only be allowed into the community of faith by converting to Judaism. So after quoting several supporting verses from the prophet Amos, he said the following: "It is my judgment, therefore, that we should not make it difficult for the Gentiles who are turning to God" (Acts 15:19).

I love that statement. I printed it and hung it in my study so I could look at it every day. From the very beginning, the church was trending toward making it difficult for people to turn to God. It was hard to leave grace alone. For many it just wasn't enough. It seems that religious people always want to complicate things. But Jesus came to make it easy. So we should take our cue from James. **The church should not make it difficult for people who are turning to God.**

Peter and James took a strong stand against complicating the gospel. They fully acknowledged the Jews' deep emotional attachments to their traditions. After all, most of their rites and rituals were instituted by God and had been a part of their religious and national identity for more than a thousand years. But the church leaders also had to acknowledge the undeniable work of God among the Gentiles.

While the leaders in Jerusalem did not want to create additional steps for the Gentiles coming to God, they did think it wise to encourage three specific behaviors for the sake of unity. And so they sent the Gentile believers the following letter:

The apostles and elders, your brothers,

To the Gentile believers in Antioch, Syria and Cilicia:

Greetings.

We have heard that some went out from us without our authorization and disturbed you, troubling your minds by what they said. So we all agreed to choose some men and send them to you with our dear friends Barnabas and Paul—men who have risked their lives for the name of our Lord Jesus Christ. Therefore we are sending Judas and Silas to confirm by word of mouth what we are writing. It seemed good to the Holy Spirit and to us not to burden you with anything beyond the following requirements: You are to abstain from food sacrificed to idols, from blood, from the meat of strangled animals and from sexual immorality. You will do well to avoid these things.

Farewell. (Acts 15:23–29)

They simplified what had become unnecessarily complicated. In doing so, grace was saved.

When the delegation from Jerusalem arrived in Antioch, the letter was read to the entire congregation. As you can imagine, it was well received. Especially by the men. No one had to become Jewish to become Christians. Gentiles could simply place their faith in a risen Messiah and be adopted into the family of God along with their Jewish brothers and sisters. It was that simple.

But unfortunately, it didn't stay that way.

By the second century, the message had become complicated again. Dozens of competing heresies and counterfeit gospels made salvation seemingly unattainable. In the fourth century, the Roman Empire adopted Christianity as the official religion, which ended government persecution but introduced extraordinary complexity.

In the eleventh century, Pope Urban II promised immediate remission of sins, which meant a substantially reduced amount of time in purgatory for all who agreed to march to the Holy Land and lay siege to the city of Jerusalem. Tens of thousands of European "Christians" took him up on the offer. Along the way, they slaughtered Muslims and Jews indiscriminately. All of this was made possible by an absurdly complex theological system that embraced values in direct conflict with the teaching of Jesus. Men would march to their deaths believing that their efforts in the name of the church would earn them a place in heaven.

All of this was repeated in the fifteenth century during what was later referred to as the Spanish Inquisition. Church leaders enriched themselves and the crown by confiscating property and wealth from those deemed heretics. Inquisitors were commissioned by the church to track down those who practiced their religion in ways not accorded by religious leaders. Thousands were tortured into confessing "sins" they never committed. In this reign of terror, preaching and teaching were almost all but discarded in exchange for torture and execution. The church adopted a policy of persecution against Jews and Muslims. Both groups were exiled and their property confiscated. An individual could be arrested for using the wrong kind of wafer during communion or failing to appear in church on certain holidays.

The sixteenth century saw the rise of the Reformation, which sought to return the church to its original, simple message of salvation by grace alone, through faith alone, in Christ alone. The Reformers worked hard to make the message of the gospel accessible to everybody. Church services were conducted in the language of the common person instead of Latin. The Bible, once chained to the pulpit and reserved for clergy alone, was translated into a variety of languages and widely distributed. But from the Protestant Reformation came dozens of denominations. Over time, many of these split and splintered. Some reunited only to split again. Other groups declared themselves nondenominational while adopting a carefully worded doctrinal statement to set them apart from other similarly formed groups.

You can't help but wonder how the simple message of God's grace could devolve into such mind-twisting complexity. No wonder people stay away from church in droves. We've done exactly what James instructed the first-century church not to do. We've made it difficult—difficult for those who want to turn to God.

But it shouldn't be that way.

It doesn't have to be that way.

~~~

As I said at the beginning of this chapter, *the church is most appealing when the message of grace is most apparent.* So in 1995 when we launched North Point Community Church, we had a very specific vision. We wanted to create a church that unchurched people loved to attend. We had this crazy notion that church isn't for church people; the church, like God's grace, is for *people* people. All people. Everybody.

We didn't know what we were doing. We didn't know if it would work. We knew we would be criticized. We knew we would make mistakes. We knew it would be messy. But we knew we had to try. I'll never forget our first organizational meeting. I knew what was on everybody's mind. *Why in the world are you starting another church in a city full of half-empty churches?* The question pretty much answered itself. Atlanta didn't need another church. Atlanta needed another *kind* of church—a church designed with unchurched people in mind.

Atlanta was and continues to be full of churches. But most of them are designed for church people. And that's okay. Church people need a place to go to church. But when church people in our part of town want to bring an unchurched friend or relative to church, it's not unusual for them to bring them to our church. I love that. I think that alone makes our church better than most other churches. By *that* I don't mean the preaching. The *that* I'm referring to is that when people ask, "Which church is best suited for my unbelieving, unchurched friend?" we come to mind first.

I don't know if it's coincidence or providence that I'm writing this chapter on a Sunday afternoon. But this morning I was sitting on the front row where I always sit, enjoying the music, when the person behind me tapped me on the shoulder and handed me a bulletin with a note scribbled on it. It was from a couple several rows back who had passed it up to me row by row. This has never happened to me before during a service. Here's what they wrote:

> Andy,
>
> Thank you for creating a church where we are comfortable bringing our unchurched friends.
>
> Don & Nikki

I got so choked up I couldn't sing. Actually, I can't really sing anyway, but that's beside the point.

Today we baptized seven people during our three morning services. To be baptized in our church, you have to let us record a three- to four-minute video of you describing your faith journey. Four out of the seven were adults who grew up in church, then dropped out after high school or college. After getting bumped around by life, they met someone who invited them to our church. Here they were, in most cases several months or a year after their first visit, in front of several thousand people, declaring that Jesus Christ is now their Lord and Savior. One guy had no church background at all. A guy at work invited him to North Point. He assured his friend that he wasn't much of a church person. His friend assured him that we weren't much of a church. So he came. Then he came back. Then he joined a Starting Point group. Eight weeks in, he gave his life to Christ. And now he was going public with his faith.

The other two were a father and daughter pair. She's fifteen and he's in his fifties. I cried like a girl as he shared how his daughter's faith came alive in our student ministry and how the changes he saw in her led him to ask her if he could go with her to church. Here he was, six months later, a new man, going public with his faith. And in case you visit, you should know that in our churches when someone comes up out of the water, we cheer. We celebrate. It's not uncommon for friends to bring posters with the name of the person they've come to see baptized written in big, bold letters. Jesus made a statement that supports our rather unruly behavior. He said, "I tell you that in the same way there will be more rejoicing in heaven over one sinner who repents than over ninety-nine righteous persons who do not need to repent" (Luke 15:7). We figure if heaven is celebrating, we should join in.

That was today. Just one Sunday in the life of one church that's working hard not to make it difficult for people who are turning to God. We don't always get it right. But it bugs the heck out of us when we don't.

~~~

Like every church, we fight the gravitational pull toward creating a church for church people. But that's a fight worth getting involved in. It's a fight more and more churches are undertaking. But I don't understand why every church wouldn't determine to become a church for unchurched people. Pardon my naiveté, boldness, arrogance, or however you choose to interpret it, but I think what we experienced today should be the norm in every gathering that calls itself a church. It's a shame that a couple had to thank their pastor for creating a church where they are comfortable bringing their unbelieving friends. Why should that be the exception and not the rule?

It's a shame that most churches are married to a designed-by-

Christians-for-Christians-only culture. A culture in which they talk about the Great Commission, sing songs about the Great Commission, but refuse to organize their church around the Great Commission. In the same way, churches talk about grace, singing about how "amazing" it is. But they create graceless cultures where only those who play by the rules feel welcomed. There's a big difference between preaching a message *about* grace and creating a community *of* grace. A *big* difference. But that is the kind of community Jesus came to create—a community that celebrates what the Father celebrates: sinners being confronted with the grace of God and being changed.

~~~

The church is God's medium for exporting, illustrating, and modeling the grace of God in the world. The church is the steward of his grace. **The church has been assigned the task of exposing our neighborhoods, communities, cities, states, and world to the grace of God. This is our mission. This is our responsibility. There is no plan B. We are it.** And we've got to get it right.

Why? Why should every local church reinvent itself around the message and offer of grace? Because, as Reuben Morgan and Ben Fielding so eloquently put it,

> Everyone *needs compassion,*
> *Love that's never failing; . . .*
> Everyone *needs forgiveness,*
> *The kindness of a Savior;*
> *The Hope of nations.*[1]

Think about it. We are stewards of the same grace poured out in the garden of Eden after sin stained every created thing. The grace that moved God to start over with a man whose descendants would become a nation that would become a blessing to all nations. It's the grace experienced by Rahab and Judah. The grace Jonah found so perplexing and that David found so comforting. It's the grace that captured the heart of a traitor like Matthew as well as a righteous man like Nicodemus. It's the grace that assured a dying criminal that—in spite of his inability to right any of his wrongs—within hours he would find himself in the presence of God.

So let's do what Jesus died to make possible. Let's heed his brother James's advice to the first church. Let's quit making it difficult for those who are turning to God. Let's make God's grace accessible to everyone.

After all, it's not your grace.

It's not my grace.

It's God's grace.

And it's for everybody.

How Sweet the Sound

While I've been writing this book, there has been a little voice in the back of my brain whispering, "But what about . . ."

"What about obedience?"

"What about disobedience?"

"What about repeated misbehavior?"

"What about bad habits?"

"What about justice?"

"What about repentance?"

So it was tempting to conclude with a chapter on the benefits of obedience and the consequences of sin. After all, we can't have people running around taking advantage of God's grace.

But I chose to ignore that little voice because all the what-abouts are irrelevant to a discussion of grace. There's no connection at all. To add *that* chapter to a book on grace would be to make this a book about something else. I'm not sure there is a word in the English vocabulary for what that would be. Perhaps *almost grace*. But almost grace is like almost true. If something is almost true, it isn't.

It's this tension that makes grace so slippery. Perhaps it's this tension that has driven churches and Christians through the centuries to add to and subtract from grace. There's something in most of us that screams, *It can't be that easy!* But as much as we want to qualify grace, it can't be qualified. It's frustrating, I know. The tension between law and grace, justice and grace, fairness and grace was a big part of the first century's struggle with the message of Jesus. But clearly he was at peace. So much so that he could say to a woman caught in adultery, "I do not condemn you. . . . From now on sin no more" (John 8:11 NASB). Translated: "You're a sinner. But I don't condemn you; I'm not going to give you what you deserve. I'm extending to you exactly what you don't deserve: grace." Jesus didn't try to balance grace and truth. He gave her a full dose of both.

This is so important. If you don't get this, you will default to a diluted form of grace that is no grace at all. With that in mind I've chosen to end with one of the most familiar of all Jesus' teachings. It was his clearest exposition on the subject of God's grace, though the term *grace* itself does not appear. It came in the form of a parable—now the most well-known of all his parables. But perhaps the most misunderstood as well. In your Bible it may be entitled The Parable of the Prodigal Son. But that's misleading. It's not a parable about a son. It's a parable about two sons. Jesus made that clear in his opening statement. This is a story about two sons who were invited to a party that neither of them was comfortable attending. As different as these two boys were, their resistance to the party stemmed from a shared misunderstanding of their father. A shared misunderstanding of grace.

~⁀⁀⁀

The circumstances surrounding the telling of the parable is the filter through which the parable should be interpreted. The good people couldn't understand why Jesus was spending so much time with the not-so-good people without first requiring them to change their ways. "This man welcomes sinners and eats with them," they grumbled (Luke 15:2).

Based on the way God had always been presented, the not-so-good people were probably a bit perplexed as well. Why would a rabbi seek them out?

You can read the parable in its entirety in Luke 15. But as you probably recall, the story climaxes with the younger, rebellious son, the prodigal, coming to his senses and heading for home. He wasn't expecting a warm reception. He certainly wasn't expecting a party. The best he could hope for was a job with the other household servants. So when his father ran to meet him, the boy gave his father his prepared speech. In telling the parable, Jesus repeats the speech twice for emphasis: "Father, I have sinned against heaven and against you. I am no longer worthy to be called your son" (Luke 15:21).

The son was absolutely correct in his assessment. But in the parable the father completely ignores his son's speech and responds as if he were a returning war hero. "But the father said to his servants, 'Quick! Bring the best robe and put it on him. Put a ring on his finger and sandals on his feet. Bring the fattened calf and kill it. Let's have a feast and celebrate'" (Luke 15:22–23).

In spite of the fact that you know how the story ends, I would invite you to pause and reflect on something you may have missed in the past. There are two different stories going on here. In some ways, they aren't even connected. Story A: A rebellious kid runs out of money and options and is forced to come home. As he evaluates what he's done, he decides he may be worth servant status, so he begs his dad for a job. Story B: A father has not seen his son in ages, catches a glimpse of him coming down the road, runs to meet him, and throws a party to celebrate his return. If you were to ask the son to tell his story, he would tell you about all the bad things he's done. What a fool he's been. If you were to ask the dad to tell you his story, he would tell you, "My son is back! I'm throwing a party."

Do you see the disconnect? Let's try this. What if the father was a friend of yours whose son's drug habit had resulted in thousands of dollars in rehab bills? Then, after dragging the family through years of pain and indebtedness, the son leaves rehab early, breaks into their house, steals his mother's jewelry, and disappears for two years. Then one Thursday afternoon you get a call from your buddy and he begs you to come over that night for a party. His son just showed up in the driveway. Now he's throwing a last-minute party to celebrate the boy's return.

Would you have a few questions? I think so. They would be *what-about* questions. You would want to know if he had really *changed*, wouldn't you? You would want to know if he was back for good. You might be tempted to suggest that your friend wait a few weeks. It would feel too early for a party, don't you think? It would if you were focused on the boy's past behavior.

Now hold that thought as we finish the parable.

The older son was a rule keeper. He did everything right. He was everything a father in that culture could hope for. When he heard his father was throwing a party for his irresponsible younger brother, he was so angry he wouldn't even come inside the house (Luke 15:28). When his father came out to find out why, the older brother gave a speech not too unlike the younger brother's. It was all about the things the younger one had done, followed by what he thought he deserved for being so faithful to his father: "Look! All these years I've been slaving for you and never *disobeyed* your *orders*. Yet you never gave me even a young goat so I could celebrate with my friends" (v. 29; emphasis added).

What follows is so powerful. This was the point of the parable. Here is grace in its rawest form. The older brother continued, "But when this son of yours who has squandered your property with prostitutes *comes home*, you kill the fattened calf for him!" (v. 30; emphasis added).

The father gave the younger son precisely what he did not deserve. And both boys were confused by that. The implication from the parable is that the father was equally confused by their reluctance to celebrate. These were two different stories about two different things. One was a story of boys trying to get what they deserved. The other was a story of a father whose son had come home.

Both boys thought the father's response should reflect what they deserved. They both thought he should take their *behavior* into account. They thought their past performance should be considered. But the father's story wasn't about behavior. His story was about something else entirely. There weren't any *what-abouts* in the father's story. What the boys had or had not done was irrelevant. We know that to be the case, based on the words Jesus put in the mouth of the father toward the end of the parable: "But we had to celebrate and be glad, because . . ." (v. 32).

Because why? Jesus, tell us why you have this imaginary father responding this way to his imaginary younger son. Why would he celebrate and why so soon? And why no mention of the inheritance he wasted and the embarrassment he caused the family? What about all that? What about it?!

"But we had to celebrate and be glad, because this brother of yours was dead and is alive again; he was lost and is found" (v. 32). That was it. End of parable. That was the answer to the question of why Jesus welcomed sinners and ate with them without requiring them to do anything first: because **God celebrates, first and foremost, restored relationships**. While we want to make it about rehabilitation, God is all about restoration. When an individual accepts God's unconditional offer of forgiveness, the party starts right then and there. It was the break with mankind in the garden that broke God's heart. So why should we be so surprised to find that he celebrates restoration?

You may have a younger-brother story. Perhaps your response to this entire book has been, *Yeah, but you don't know what I've done. You don't know what kind of person I am.* You may have an older-brother story. Perhaps you've been arguing with me the whole way through. May even have put this book down a couple of times with no intention of finishing. You feel as though I'm letting everybody off too easily. You want me to be more balanced. I understand. I understand way more than you may imagine.

～◞

But Jesus said there is a third story. The father's story. God's story. In his story, he's not impressed with or distressed over what you've done or what you think other people ought to be doing. In his story those things are completely irrelevant.

In God's story, *you* are the focus of a celebration. Not what you've done. *You.*

You were lost and have been found. You were dead, and now you are alive. You were blind, and now you see. You said yes to his offer of grace. That's the best news God will ever receive about you.

In your story you are going to continue searching for a reason God should love you. In your story you are going to continue finding reasons he shouldn't. So here's my suggestion: give up your version of your story and embrace his.

In his story, he loves you no matter what you've done.

In his story, he doesn't love you because of what you've done.

In his story, he could not love you more and he will never love you less.

It's a better story.
It's a true story.
It's a story of grace.
The grace of God!

Notes

Chapter 1: In the Beginning, Grace

1. Dr. Richard Dawkins, *The God Delusion* (New York: Houghton Mifflin Harcourt, 2008), 51.
2. *Merriam-Webster's Collegiate Dictionary*, 11th edition (Springfield, MA: 2003), s.v. "mercy."

Chapter 5: Ruled by Grace

1. Benjamin Franklin, *The Writings of Benjamin Franklin*, vol. 9, ed. Albert Henry Smyth (New York: Macmillan, 1907), 569.

Chapter 6: Rescued by Grace

1. "Joshua Fought the Battle of Jericho," traditional Negro spiritual, public domain.

Chapter 7: Sustained by Grace

1. "Grace Greater Than Our Sin," words by Julia H. Johnston, public domain.

Chapter 10: Reborn by Grace

1. Alfred Edersheim, *The Life and Times of Jesus the Messiah*, vol. 2 (Grand Rapids: Eerdmans, 1962), 11.
2. *Babylonian Talmud*, Tractate Sabbat, 31a.

Chapter 12: Saved by Grace

1. Philip Yancey, *What's So Amazing About Grace?* (Grand Rapids: Zondervan, 2002), 62.
2. C. S. Lewis, *The Abolition of Man* (New York: Macmillan, 1947).

Chapter 13: Commissioned for Grace

1. "Mighty to Save," lyrics by Ben Fielding and Reuben Morgan, copyright 2006 Hillsong Publishing. Used by permission. Emphasis added.

About the Author

Andy Stanley is a pastor, communicator, author, and the founder of North Point Ministries, Inc. (NPM). Since its inception in 1995, North Point Ministries has grown from one campus to three in the Atlanta area and has helped plant eighteen strategic partner churches throughout the United States. Each Sunday, more than twenty thousand adults attend worship services at one of NPM's three campuses, North Point Community Church, Browns Bridge Community Church, and Buckhead Church. Andy's books include *It Came from Within, Communicating for a Change, Making Vision Stick, How Good Is Good Enough?, The Principle of the Path*, and *Next Generation Leader*. Andy lives in Alpharetta, Georgia, with his wife, Sandra, and their three children.

NOT WHERE YOU WANT TO BE?
WONDERING HOW TO GET THERE?

As you are about to discover, the principle of the path is at work in your life every single day. Once embraced, this compelling principle will empower you to identify and follow the path that leads to your desired destination. And this same principle will enable you to avoid life-wasting detours along the way.

"If you're ready to break the bad habits, bad behaviors, and bad decisions that have been leading you into trouble, you need Andy Stanley's *The Principle of the Path*."
—DAVE RAMSEY, HOST OF *The Dave Ramsey Show* AND BEST-SELLING AUTHOR OF *The Total Money Makeover*

Available Wherever Books Are Sold
www.thomasnelson.com